HOW TO HAVE
THE BEST TRAINED
GUN DOG

JOAN BAILEY

SWAN VALLEY PRESS

PORTLAND, OREGON

Published by:
Swan Valley Press
9601 NW Leahy Rd, Ste 209
Portland, OR 97229-6343

Publisher's Cataloging-in-Publication
(Provided by Quality Books, Inc.)

Bailey, Joan.
    How to have the best trained gun dog / Joan Bailey.
-- 1st ed.
    p. cm.
    LCCN 2008905896
    ISBN-13: 978-0-9630127-5-3
    ISBN-10: 0-9630127-5-4

    1. Hunting dogs. 2. Hunting dogs--Training.
I. Title.

SF428.5.B277 2008   636.752
                    QBI08-600203

Cover Design: Another Jones Graphics, Portland, Oregon
Cover Photo: Joe Schmutz
Photographs: Ed Bailey unless noted
Printed by: United Graphics, Matoon, Illinois
To order Toll Free: 1-866-296-6725

www.swanvalleypress.com

Dedicated To

Jack Dallimore

WARNING—DISCLAIMER

CONTENTS

Photo 1. *This is proof of why we want our dogs to be fully trained. She is a Large Munsterlander (one of the versatile breeds from Germany), SUNNYNOOK'S IBIS, grandmother of SORA on the cover. The goose was shot by Joe Schmutz at a lake near Saskatoon. Joe and his wife, Sheila, are active in the L.M. Club of N.A. (Compliments Joe Schmutz.)*

ACKNOWLEDGMENTS

In the early stages of this book, when a glimmer of the idea was forming, I sent four rough chapters and an outline to a few long-time colleagues to ask, "Is this a book?" These friends are Larry Mueller, hunting dog editor *Outdoor Life*, Jack Dallimore, long time judge of versatile dogs, Dennis Carlson, also an experienced field judge, Ken Osborn, professional trainer, John Lundberg, experienced and well read on the subject of dogs and their behavior, Warren Webster, long time field judge, and Phil Bennett, an astute observer of dogs, and a field judge. They all answered, "Yes. Write it." With encouragement I wrote.

Jack, Phil, and Dennis read many versions of this book, many rewrites. These friends and colleagues gave me their precious time out of busy working lives to read the manuscript many times. They helped me to articulate my ideas in such a way that the reader can understand easily how to use this down to earth method to make your gun dog be better than you could have ever imagined.

When the book was well along, after perhaps 12 or 15 rewrites, I asked a friend, John McGonigle, to read the manuscript. He is flushing dog columnist for *Gun Dog* magazine, and *Upland Almanac* magazine. He is outdoors editor for *Lancaster Sunday News* in Pennsylvania and other outdoor publications. Talk about time, John spent a great amount of his time editing the manuscript. He tightened my prose throughout, made suggestions which he always followed with his "or not," giving me freedom to use it or not. His input made a huge difference in this book.

Other readers are both long-time friends: each helped me with my previous books, and read for me again here. My thanks once again to Kohel Haver and Brad Meyen.

At the end I asked Jim Seibel to read for me. He is another excellent field judge with a lot of experience in this subject. What the others did for me at the start, Jim did the same at the finish line, as did Phil. Jim's support and suggestions were vital to the completion of this work.

Jack Dallimore was a rock for me. He gave me constant, lasting support. He was there for me from the very beginning to the end, always with wisdom about this subject. Not only does Jack understand dogs, but he also understands the dog owners. Over and over he got inside the mind of the owner, and thus helped me strive for clarity.

I am forever grateful to these friends, who know and understand this fascinating subject. I thank them for their encouragement and input for this book.

CHAPTER ONE

How This Unique Sequence Works

THERE ARE MANY METHODS for training a gun dog. What follows is a combination of methods that are easy for me to use and are successful in producing a fully trained gun dog—a dog that I can control in any hunting situation as well as in any day-to-day family life.

Basics

For the basics I start with methods used in Europe for decades that involve little or no pain. Then I add a combination of methods learned in my early participation in NAVHDA (North American Versatile Hunting Dog Association). Much of this came from working with Bodo Winterhelt in the early years of NAVHDA including preparing my dog for the Utility Field Test (for the fully trained versatile hunting dog) and then as a judge for NAVHDA, the WPGCA (Wirehaired Pointing Griffon Club of America), and the KDK (Klub Deutsch Kurzhaar, translated from German to German Shorthair Club).

Decades of judging with talented people seemed almost like getting a master's degree from Harvard or Yale! The best and most important teachers though, were all the dogs. If you watch enough of them, they will teach you.

Sequence

The training sequence here starts with the translation of three chapters of a training book from Germany: *Der Jagdgebraunchshund* (The All Purpose Hunting Dog) by Dr. Carl Tabel, first published in Germany in 1964. A new edition came out in 1974, with more editions up to the present. These training methods have worked for gun dog owners for more than 60 years and still going strong today.

It was some years ago when I had the great good fortune to meet Dr. Tabel's son, Henry. I had a young Griffon about four or five months old. Henry recognized the breed and told me about his father. Soon he brought a copy of his father's training book and showed us the relevant photos and the step-by-step exercises. We found someone to translate the training sections relevant to hunting in North America. By the time the translation was completed, my young dog was nine months old and I began the training. And it worked, as it has for thousands of hunters over many decades.

As editor (and secretary) of the WPGCA newsletter I published the translations of the three basic chapters from Dr. Tabel's book in our newsletter, one chapter per issue. For those chapters we carefully studied the original photos, then took new, more up-to-date pictures that demonstrated each step to accompany each article. A few years later when NAVHDA published their "Green Book" (*The Training and Care of the Versatile Hunting Dog),* the WPGCA gave NAVHDA permission to use two of our translated articles from the WPGCA newsletters in their new book. NAVHDA included parts of the article on Obedience and the entire article on Drop using our photos.

Understanding the foundation for this training program

I use Dr. Tabel's basic obedience chapter, his force retrieving, and his "drop" as the foundation for training my dog. All of these training methods are based on Dr. Tabel's underlying philosophy that the dog does what he is told not only because he likes to do it and because he likes to please you, but also because the dog understands that he must do it. If you have a dog that likes to retrieve and you never had an opportunity to make him retrieve, inevitably the day will come when he simply decides he doesn't feel like going into the cold water to get the duck. And there you are, with no means to get the duck except by wading in cold water, perhaps up to your waist, or worse; letting wounded game escape or dead game go to waste.

The fully trained hunting dog guarantees that you will have a better hunting dog and that you will find more game and put more game in your bag, thanks to the teamwork between you and your trained dog. You will also have a safe dog because you can stop him anywhere. For example, if you are on one side of a dirt road, and the dog is on the other but is about to run over to you with a car coming around a bend, you can simply give the command "Drop" and your fully trained dog will stop. You saved his life.

Another perk that comes with a fully trained hunting dog is that you also have a fully trained family dog. Having company? Tell the dog to stay on his spot in the corner, on his little piece of rug or mat. Despite people walking past him, talking, laughing, and eating, the dog will remain there until you release him to walk around among your guests. This will astound your guests! In Europe, especially in Germany and France, dogs are allowed to accompany their owners into many public areas including restaurants because their dogs are conditioned and trained to lie under or beside the table.

When to Start This Training

The type of training used in this book should not be done until the dog is at least 9 months old and has gone through his first hunting season (as described in *How to Help Gun Dogs Train Themselves*). The training here puts emotional pressure on the dog, so you want the dog to be emotionally developed enough so that he can go through the training without caving in or going sour on you. His first hunting season will provide just that. So the end of his first hunting season is an ideal time to start the program. Even if it's December or January you can do a lot of the basic stuff in the basement, garage, and fenced in yard.

Caution

If you have a dog that's a little "soft," you can still use this training method *if the dog has a strong desire to please you,* **AND** *a strong desire to find game.* These two traits can almost always overcome a dog that is a bit soft—say shy of strangers. *But if the dog is extremely soft he will probably collapse under this pressure. With a lot of patience you may be able to adapt some of the training for a soft dog.*

You can easily tell if a dog is soft if he is timid about any strange people, new places, strange noises, if he is hyper, or if as a young pup he was a "piddler." (That means if a strange person came into the house, he would squat and pee.) These are all symptoms of a soft dog.

During the months preceding training it's essential that you have built up a close relationship with your dog, through all the informal conditioning and exposure you have provided since you got your pup. The dog must feel close to you, and have deep affection for you. And you must understand your dog's personality. *If you haven't done this work you should not attempt the type of training in this book.*

This book also assumes that: 1) You have purchased a well bred dog from a reputable breeder, and that the dog is mentally and physically sound. (See *How to Help Gun Dogs Train Themselves* to learn how to find such a breeder.) 2) Your dog is not soft, not overly aggressive, and not hyper in any way.

Your Commitment is Ten Minutes a Day

It's essential that you make a commitment for a chunk of time for three to four consecutive months. Needing only ten minutes a day is an easy commitment to keep. Check your calendar and be sure you can start the training and carry it through. Every dog and every trainer are different so we don't know exactly how long it will be until your dog is fully trained. Plan on several consecutive months, during a period when the weather is decent enough to work outside at least most of the time.

How Often to Have a Training Session

Once training is started, twice a day is good, once a day is mandatory for chapters 2, 3, and 4. Each training session is very short—10 minutes plus prep time, and fun time. So if you want to do one session in the morning before you go to work, get up 30 minutes earlier. You won't be working with the dog for 30 minutes, but you want that time to quiet yourself and think about what you are going to do with your dog that day.

Important: *End every training session on a positive note.* If the dog has not done a step successfully, go back to the step he has done successfully, either during this session, or yesterday's session. Then you can end on a positive note, with a "good boy." At the end of every training session release your dog verbally ("okay," "come," or whatever your release word is) from "training" and bend over and rough house a little bit. Maybe run around the yard together. *This is a vital part of this training. Don't forget to do this.*

You may think playing is silly, but it's not; it's important in building the relationship between you and your dog. It means that when you have to be tough on your dog he will still think of you as someone he likes and still wants to be with and please you.

Always remove the pinch collar at the end of each session and put on the dog's regular collar. He will come to learn that the pinch collar means he is going to work.

The actual training session is only 10 minutes, but you must set aside 30 minutes so that there is calm before you start, and a little warmth and play at the end. After an evening session, if there is time and daylight, a run, even a short one (10 minutes), can be the best reward for your dog.

Imagine how you'll feel in the morning after your 30 minutes devoted to your dog as you drive off to work! What a way to start your day! And your dog will quickly become used to your "daily appointment" with him and will look forward to it.

If you want to do two sessions a day, set aside 30 minutes in the evening, for the same routine. Or, you can do one training session a day. You can feel your way on this and decide how to do it. Maybe some days you will do one session and another day two sessions.

Overall Training Information

Most dogs enjoy this training, though at times it is a bit tough on them. But dogs love to work, they love having a job to do, and if they were brought up properly during the first 16 weeks of their lives they *developed a lifelong desire to learn.* Training for them is enjoyable and interesting. When you have two dogs and you take one for a training session, the other one is always jealous and the one being trained feels special.

A final word of caution: Up to this point in your dog's life, things have been pretty rosy. Other than learning good manners and to come, and what no means and what whoa means, there has not been a great deal of pressure for your dog. He's been having a good time, going on outings, going for runs, learning a little about using his nose, searching for game, and maybe doing some natural retrieving if the opportunity arises. And he has already had his first hunting season.

When you begin this serious training it will be a bit of a shock to the dog. Be sure when you first exert firmness that you do it with kindness and in a way that the dog will not become afraid. Commands should usually be given in a quiet, normal voice, but with firmness. A benevolent trainer is the best trainer.

This book is written for a right-handed person. If you are left-handed you may want to go through the entire book and change that aspect to suit yourself.

It's a good idea to read the book straight through. Then go back and read it again, highlighting the places you think are important for you and your dog.

General Tips and Reminders

(Some of these are in the text as well.)

1. When I start formal training with a young dog, I have to read over the next day's work the night before. And the next day I read it again just before I go out to work with him. For me it helps me remember all the little important details. This might not be necessary for a lot of you, but it is an option.

2. Always stop a training session while the dog still wants to do more, not when he is tired or bored.

3. If you're in a bad mood, angry at someone, upset about something at work, or worried about anything major, it's not a good time to have a training session with your dog. Your dog will know something is wrong, because, like kids, dogs know everything. Both you and the dog will be unable to give the lesson 100 percent concentration. Instead of a lesson, just take yourself and the dog out for a good run. You'll both feel better, and then the next training session will go a lot better. A day off never hurt anyone.

4. Keep most of the training sessions short—10 minutes, no longer.

5. Dr. Tabel says, "Only repetition will make the dog respond as if it were a habit." Pro trainer Ken Osborn says it this way: "Repetition, repetition until it becomes a habit, and then it becomes the behavior." This from two fine trainers who know what they are talking about.

6. Throughout the training remember to "read" your dog. Observe him as he goes about learning each step. An example:

After eight minutes of work (training) is he beginning to wilt? Is his tail drooping a bit? Is his head hanging down? Are his eyes focused, or are they starting to glaze over a bit? These would be signs that the dog has had all the training he can take for this session—you probably should have stopped sooner. Stay aware of how your dog feels as you go through every training session. *Keep reading your dog.*

7. End every training session by doing four things:

   • End with success, on a positive note, followed by praise.

   • Release you dog by giving it a command that means: "Okay, you can walk around."

   • Play and rough house with your dog a little.

   • Go for a run if possible.

8. Our body language is critical for training a dog: "...dogs seem to remember silhouettes, i.e., when a dog takes a hand signal he will remember what it means if he sees his boss with one arm pointing out to his side; it's the pattern that he sees and remembers. If we think just a bit about how wolves take down their prey (which they must do to survive), they work together *never uttering a sound,* but they communicate by body movements; every part of their body becomes a vessel in which to send a message: go faster, hold back, slow down, come this way, go closer, all done without a sound. Yet their posture, their ears, their tails are constantly sending messages." (Page 203 *How To Help Gun Dogs Train Themselves.*)

So without being conscious of it we are constantly sending messages to our dog through our own body movements. We often think that our dog can read our mind; perhaps he's reading our body. It's a good idea to understand this as you work with your dog. See the bibliography for books that cover this subject in depth.

9. "As you proceed through your training program remember to use the commands on a daily basis as a means of reinforcing all the lessons. For example, when you are taking your dog out to the field to do some training such as the drag track, be sure you are consistent with all the previous things your dog has learned: sit, heel, fetch, come, etc. Whatever he's learned, keep using it so he doesn't forget. The trained dog will *always* require exercising the training to keep the dog dependable in all future training and in all future work." *Jack Dallimore*

Essential Equipment

You must have all the necessary equipment. See the Appendix for companies that carry these items.

1. **Over-the-shoulder leash.** Either leather or web. This leash frees both hands while you and the dog are walking, and makes it easier for you to carry your gun while the dog is on leash walking at heel. It frees you a great deal during training. For example, you'll need a free hand to carry the switch during the sit-and-stay training. The leash has several snaps which allow it to be used in many ways in the field. The leather leash is nice and quite usable, but the web is less expensive and more practical when the fields are wet and during the beginning part of water retrieving training. (Some companies call this a "Jaeger leash." Jaeger means hunter in German.)

2. **Pinch (or prong) metal collar.** This is a metal choke collar with blunt prongs. The philosophy behind this type of collar is that when the dog is punished by a quick upward movement, the prongs "grab" around the dog's neck, which is exactly what happens when dogs fight, or when as pups their mothers grabbed them by the neck. This collar produces a sensation of submissive feeling and puts the trainer in the dominant position. *Without this collar this entire method of training will not work.*

Use the pinch collar only during training sessions. When you put the collar on the dog he will know it's time for "work." When you remove it after the training session he will know it's time to play and go for a run.

3. **Long Leash or Line.** About 30 feet.

4. **Whistle.** This should be the two tone whistle as used originally in Germany. They were made of elk horn. There is one sold in the U.S. made of buffalo horn (Lion Country Supply). One end has a very loud trill; the other end has a softer tweet. You will need to use both ends. The softer end is a "tweet." I like two short tweets, or peeps, for "come." The other end (rounded) produces a loud trill, and is used only for the "Drop," when you stop your dog wherever he is. Important tip: *Buy two whistles.* Keep one in the glove compartment of your car or pickup. That's insurance for the day you get out in the field, or on a hunting trip and you forgot your whistle.

5. **Thin, light switch (See Photos 3 and 5, Chapter 2.)**

6. **Light wooden dummy. (See photo 3, Chapter 4.)**

7. **Stuffed skins of quail, chukar, pheasant, duck.** You'll have to make them yourself.

8. **Dummy that allows you to add weights in small increments for the retrieving work.**

9. **Fenced back yard.**

10. **A daylight basement.** Even a regular basement is usable for the initial steps of obedience training. A garage works (as long as there are no harmful chemicals or dangerous tools). If there's a blizzard outside you can still have a session in the basement.

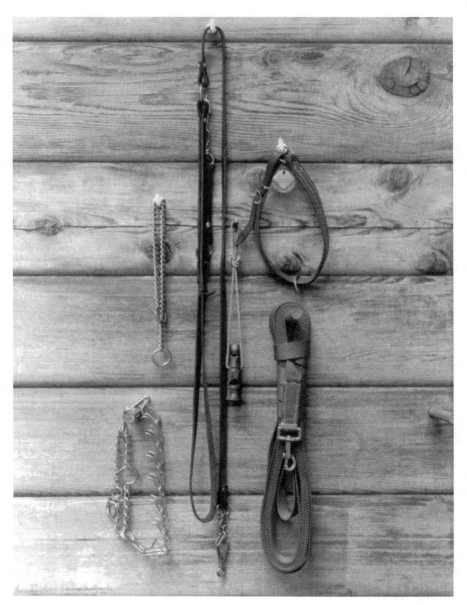

Photo 1. *Chain choke collar, over-the-shoulder leash, leather collar (or a web collar works just as well), pinch collar, two-tone whistle, 30 foot long line.*

CHAPTER TWO

Obedience: Sit and Stay
The Foundation

When to begin

Do not start this training until after your dog's first hunting season. This gives the young dog more time for conditioning, more exposure, and most importantly, exposure in learning what he was bred to do—hunt. Having this positive, happy hunting season is the best foundation for starting your dog's formal training in order to build a great gun dog. Remember, the first hunting season is all about what is best for *him*, not about how many birds you bring home each day.

Begin the training program after the first hunting season, when the dog is at least 9 months old. At this point the dog is a little like a pre-teen in human life. At two years the dog is a full blown teenager and that's a whole different ball game. But having a completely trained dog by the time he is two years old, gives you a much greater edge for getting through the "terrible twos." (See *The Awkward Age, This Too Shall Pass* in the appendix of *How To Help Gun Dogs Train Themselves.*)

Training your dog after his first hunting season makes the training easier for several reasons: his maturity, experience in hunting, and a stronger bond with you because you and he went through the hunting season together.

13

Preparing for Training

How to use the pinch collar

Be sure you buy the correct size collar. This type of collar should not be too loose or it will not do the job it was designed to do. It should fit in a similar manner as a regular collar—not too loose (you should be able to get two fingers under the collar when it's on the dog, but no more than that). The collar comes with extra links so you can adjust the size to make the perfect fit. You unclip a link to put the collar on your dog and you remove the collar the same way by unclipping a link.

Never use a steady pull because it will not give a signal to your dog. Instead, use short, very light, quick flicks in the beginning when the dog is just getting used to the collar. For example, the first day of the first lesson of "sit," you'll want to keep the dog's head up by using the leash. So use it in a gentle upward flick, almost a reminder for the dog. Same for the first lessons of "come" and "heeling." After the first or second lesson the dog will be accustomed to the collar which is similar to a mother dog correcting a pup—she gives it a *quick grab* and then either releases it in a few moments, or carries it somewhere. This is usually all the pup needs to realize he shouldn't be doing whatever he was doing. So a quick, *light flick* and immediately a release.

Training Tip: *Try the pinch collar on the dog a week before you start the training. The first day of training you don't want to have to be fiddling around with the collar, removing links, or adding links. The "fitting"* should be done at least a week before you start training. Then every other day put the collar on for just a minute or two, then remove it. *Do this the week before your training program begins.*

Of utmost importance with this training program is that you do it in very small steps. Patience is required of the trainer—that means you. This is the very thing that makes this training easier, no giant steps, just baby steps.

The "Sit"

1. **Training Place:** Inside a fenced yard, or basement, empty garage (with no hazardous equipment or liquids like anti-freeze, which is poisonous and animals like to drink it.) and later outside with distractions.

2. **Equipment:** Pinch collar, short and long leashes, small light-weight switch.

3. **Sequence of Training for the Sit:**

   1) Right hand holds the short leash; left hand is pressed on kidney region. Then give command to "sit."
   2) Command intensification (instead of pushing with left hand, use the switch lightly on the rump. *See below for important information on the use of the switch*).
   3) Let the dog sit for 30 seconds; hold up the line, circle dog.
   4) Call "come" (or "here") or give quiet whistle encouragement.
   5) Repeat the sit, this time for 60 seconds; hold up line, circle dog.
   6) Repetition of steps with interchanges of "sit."
   7) "Sit," drop line. Trainer leaves the dog. Quiet whistle with command "come."
   8) Length of each exercise: 10 minutes maximum. *This is very important. Do not work the dog on these steps for more than 10 minutes.*

Step 1. *The dog has the pinch collar on and the short leash is used.*

Hold the leash in your right hand just behind the collar so that it's a short distance (about one foot) from the collar, and keep your hand above the dog's head. Your left hand touches the dog with spread fingers around his kidney region. (See Photo 1.) At the command "sit," give a short, quick, soft, upward flick of the leash (not too hard, more like a signal to the dog) with the right hand to avoid the possibility of the dog lying down. It's just enough to keep his head up. At the same time your left hand pushes the dog down, forcing him to sit. If the dog does this obediently, praise the dog immediately with a soft "good boy." After approximately 30-60 seconds the trainer gives the command "come" and walks around with the dog a little. After three to five repetitions of Step 1 the dog should understand that he has to sit on command.

Now do the exercise without the left hand pushing him down. It is essential to start over at the beginning if the dog does not understand at this point. It has to be practiced until the dog will sit for one minute in front of his trainer, without the dog trying to get up. Usually after 10 minutes the dog will understand. Then take a short forward step on your left foot, and give a clear command, "come;" your dog is forced to get up and go toward you. A short, light signal on the leash might also be needed.

Photo 1. *Firm pressure on the kidneys with your fingertips makes the dog sit. Keep his head up by holding the leash straight up with your right hand to prevent the dog from lying down.*

Step 2. *We now use a thin switch like a willow switch as an aid.*

How to use the switch

The switch is used with a quick tap that is just hard enough to get the dog's attention, but does not harm him, or frighten him. It's a quick flick; more of a reminder than a punishment. But it's necessary because it can reach the dog when you can't reach him with your hand. (See Photos 2 and 3.)

I always practice with the switch before I start the training program, to make sure I know exactly how hard, or how soft I need to use it. I go outside *without the dog* and practice by hitting the palm of my hand, or my thigh. I do it several times to make sure that I will not hurt the dog, but hard enough to be uncomfortable in order to get his attention.

Photo 2. *The dog should see the switch and demonstrate complete attention to you while you walk around him.*

The switch is like a stern reminder—when I say "sit" I mean "sit now." It's kind of an extension of you, the Boss, yet although your hand is not touching the dog, he will get the message quickly. And timing is everything, so that's why I practice without the dog, so that I'm confident I know exactly how to use it the way it was intended—a *quick light tap* to reinforce the command.

Step 2 begins with the dog understanding that he is supposed to sit down at the command "sit." Instead of using your hand to push the dog down, you now use the switch. If the dog is slow to respond to the command, the trainer gives a quick, light tap on the dog's rump, repeating the command "sit." It has to be hard enough to be uncomfortable, but never causes severe pain. That's why you must practice on yourself until you are confident that you won't harm the dog. *It is very important now for the trainer to react very quickly in giving the dog his penalty if necessary, or to encourage and reward when necessary.* The dog will understand quickly by the correct instructions. It is possible that the dog will try to lie down, which is to be prevented by one, quick, short upward pull of the leash, followed by an immediate release when the dog complies.

Usually this exercise is learned successfully on the first day, though it is not important how long it takes. It is very important that this step is understood before progressing to the next exercise. So if it takes two consecutive days that's okay. *Remember, that the actual length of time of the lesson is 10 minutes,* ending on a positive note, with a little playing.

Step 3. *"Sit" and remaining at the sit while trainer moves around.*

Place the dog in the sit position. Stand in front of the dog with the switch in your right hand. Hold the leash in your left hand. With a pointed finger, look the dog straight and sharply in the eyes. After the command "sit," step to the side. Any attempt by the dog to get up is answered with a repeated "sit" command and a swift tap with the switch. If the dog remains sitting; increase your distance. After a while step behind him.

Since the dog cannot see you he will understandably try to get up. It is essential to hold the switch above the dog's head so he can still see it. Usually this exercise is learned after the second exercise day. *Gradually increase the time of the sitting to 5 minutes.* End the exercise with the command "come," followed by encouragement, reward, praise—and then a run. This may take two or three training sessions.

Step 4. *The "sit" while the trainer stops walking—the dog sits when you stop without being told.*

Start walking with the dog at heel while you hold the leash loosely in your left hand, or hanging over your shoulder. Hold the switch in your right hand behind your back so you can reach his rump. (See Photo 3.) Stop suddenly, stand still and say "sit," followed immediately by a quick tap on the dog's rump. The dog will sit as he has learned. Probably the hit or tap will be into space, because the dog sits before he is tapped. If he does not sit after the command and tap, use the switch again and at the same time give a quick, light pull up on the leash. This brings his head up and gets him starting to sit.

Photo 3. *Stop walking, say "sit" and immediately use the switch to tap the dog's rump.*

Give the command "heel" and continue walking 10 or 20 steps. Stop and immediately repeat this exercise—"sit." The dog is now learning the first part of heeling, and also that he must always sit when the handler stops walking. Do this exercise often until the dog is sitting automatically when you stop, without the need of a command or use of the switch.

Next do the same exercise out in a field or you can start on your front lawn and progress to the field. The purpose here is that when the dog is at heel, he sits when you stop no matter where he is and despite any distractions like a robin flying up, or someone walking down your sidewalk. Stopping and standing still is always the signal for the dog to sit.

Step 5. *"Sit" and "come" on voice command or soft whistle.*

The dog is sitting with the long line attached to the dog's collar. Walk 6-10 yards from the dog say "come," while waving your other hand from straight up in the air downward until your hand touches your thigh. With the other hand gently pull the line. When the dog comes to you say "sit," and *instantly* give him a lot of praise!

After doing this step *successfully* 3-5 times, leave out the verbal command "come" and replace it with the whistle—two quick, short peeps using the thin end of the whistle. (Don't whistle too loudly because you are so close to the dog.) You are getting the dog used to the whistle, which will become his command to always come to you. Later we will use a strong, long blast on the other end of the whistle for the dog to "drop," but that's a long way off. (In actual hunting conditions your dog may be out of sight and you will give those two short peeps as loudly as you can so your dog can hear you.) In this training situation, however, the peeps should be soft.

Two soft toots, a wave with the right arm, and perhaps a pull on the line, will call the dog to you. Soon the pull on the line or the wave of the arm will not be necessary. He will come willingly on the double whistle to get his reward ("good boy" and maybe a quick pat). He probably learned this earlier in life as a pup when you were conditioning him in the field, but it's good to put him through this now, while using more discipline. This is a little like a refresher course with more pressure and more expectations on your part.

Don't over use the whistle during this training. If you use it too much the dog will start to come to you without waiting for the command. If this ever happens then you must go back and repeat Exercise 3. The dog must learn that he may only leave where he is sitting after a command—the whistle, voice or wave of the hand. *This is important for the more advanced training in later chapters, so be sure he learns it well now.*

Step 6. *"Sit" according to steps 2-5 in the field with distraction.*

The dog clearly understands the command "sit." (The handler standing still, maybe pointing your finger.) These are signals for the dog that he must sit immediately and stay sitting. By doing your training on a daily basis the dog should be able to do this in 3-5 days. While doing this the dog is also learning to *concentrate* on his BOSS, which is the most important thing of all. In the field the dog will have to prove his obedience with many distractions (such as flying birds, strange people and other dogs).

Repeat all of these exercises (2 to 5) in the yard using the long line so that the dog is used to the long line before you go in the field. In the field the line prevents the dog from running away and keeps the dog from losing respect for the BOSS. (Boss gives commands— the dog obeys.)

Then go to the field and repeat steps 1 to 5. You will now deliberately bring in distractions of all kinds such as tossing a stick, or waving a cloth in front of him. *He must remain sitting.* (You may need a helper for the distractions, someone who thoroughly understands what you are trying to accomplish.)

Be sure you go to different field areas so that the dog understands he has to obey the command anywhere, and so he doesn't get bored.

At first keep the dog on the long line. Once he is performing well *on all tasks with distractions,* quietly unsnap the leash from the collar and continue, starting with Step 1, working up to Step 5. So: sit, then sit while Boss moves around, heel beside Boss, sit when Boss stops, and coming to Boss on the command "come." Do these steps at a short distance away from the dog, then gradually increase the distance. Step 6 will take several days. If the dog makes a mistake, or fails to obey a command, correct him and go on. Then go back to the previous lesson that he did correctly, where he will succeed so that you can end on a positive note.

This is hard work for a nine month-old dog. That's why it's critical to restrict training sessions to 10 minutes. If he hasn't had proper exposure during the first nine months of his life (as described in *How To Help Gun Dogs Train Themselves*), or if he hasn't gone through his first hunting season, he might cave in under this pressure. Again, it's best not to start this training until after the dog's first hunting season and until he is at least nine months old.

Tip

When I start the formal training with a young dog, I read over the next step, or the next day's work, the night before and again the next day just before I start working with him. It helps me to remember all the little details that are so important. This might not be necessary for most of you, but it's an option.

CHAPTER THREE

Obedience Part Two: Leash Training and Heeling

To SOME EXTENT your dog has already learned that "heel" means to stay by your left knee and it's uncomfortable if he doesn't (the pricking of the pinch collar). Now we will extend this to learning many conditions where he is required to stay next to your left knee—sometimes walking and sometimes sitting. This is a continuation of the foundation for this training program.

Step 1.

Leash training and heeling are best done in a basement, garage, or fenced yard. The dog wears the pinch collar and you are using the short, over-the-shoulder leash. The dog is on your left side. You are near a wall of some sort (basement wall, garage wall or fence). Hold the leash loosely in your left hand to give it a little play. At first it has no purpose other than to be a guide. Don't change the leash's position, with one exception; the line may be loosened if the dog gets frightened.

When you give the verbal command "heel," step out with your left leg, which will be a visual signal to the dog. If you step out with your right leg, he will always be a little behind you and will try to catch up. Remember, *left leg first* when starting the heeling lesson.

You can encourage the dog—pat your left thigh, say "come" if necessary. Hold the leash in your right hand with 12-16 inches of play for the dog, use the command heel and walk at a slow pace either forward or backward along the wall. (See Photo 1 and 2.) Normally the dog will follow obediently. Walk along the wall, or fence, so closely that a sideways movement for him is impossible.

Photo 1. *Proper way to hold the leash while walking dog at heel. Notice how the left hand holds the leash close to the collar for quick correction if needed, or to loosen if the dog becomes frightened, especially in the beginning.*

Photo 2. *Encourage your dog to come along by slapping your thigh and urging him with your voice.*

The dog is between the wall and you. You can expect that the dog will follow your command because of the pinch collar. However, he might try to lie down when he feels the pricking of the collar. This is when you must remain calm. Wait until he calms down and stands up again. Even on the first training day the young dog will understand that by being obedient the collar will not hurt him. If he follows you but is afraid or unwilling, encourage him but don't stand still. Keep walking (see Photo 2.).

Once the dog has walked with you for 30-40 yards, turn right and go back, so he must catch up to you. He will probably hurry to get ahead. It would be wrong to hinder him by pulling on the leash because the purpose of the exercise is to train him to follow at his Boss's left knee. So, when he tries to push ahead, you must quickly step to the left and onto his paw, *which is why you must wear soft tennis shoes or other soft shoes for this.* (See Photo 3.) If he tries to escape to the side a quick pull on the leash will correct him. Petting him will do wonders if he is afraid. In this way you'll help him concentrate and learn very quickly.

Photo 3. *Use soft tennis shoes for heeling training. When the dog attempts to pull ahead, stride to the left a little, stepping lightly on his feet. This teaches him to keep his attention on you.*

Pushing your knee or leg will not do much good. The dog must learn that if he walks in front of, or ahead of his Boss's knee, he will become uncomfortable. Usually after a dog has been stepped on three times, the intelligent dog will concentrate on his Boss and jump towards the left on his own. Even if he tries to escape backward, forward, or sideways, keep on walking to make him understand that any "escape" will hurt.

The walking has to be altered 10, 20, 30 yards along the wall, across the room, then to the left, suddenly walk faster, then slow again. Keep changing direction and pace. It's essential that you react immediately to any wrong move the dog makes.

Remember, at this point training sessions should not be more than 10 minutes. Later, when the dog is more familiar with the commands like "sit," "heel," "drop," and "fetch," the length of exercise time can *sometimes* be extended to 15 or 20 minutes *when you are working in the field.* In any case stop the exercise (always on a positive note) if the dog shows signs of being tired.

It doesn't matter if it takes several days to do these first steps. A lot depends on the individual dog—his intelligence, desire to please, and his age. The inexperienced trainer may take a little longer than a seasoned one. The most important point of all is that *the dog learns each step thoroughly.* This will reduce your time later on, because the basics will be fully in place.

Step 2. *Heeling and sit outdoors and in the field.*

Once the dog is performing the previous steps well in the basement, garage or fenced yard, change to outdoor training. Fences and trees of any size will take the place of a wall. Walk by all the obstacles without stopping. The dog must pass each obstacle on the same side you do. (See Photo 4.) The location and the speed you walk should be changed often, because the intelligent dog will soon get to know every obstacle. Walk on sidewalks, use a fenced school yard when not in use.

Walk in a normal manner; allow the dog to make a mistake and let him figure it out himself. If he has any trouble guide him slightly so he begins to learn how to walk close to your knee no matter what. Be patient and stay engaged. In the beginning you may have to guide him closer to the tree a bit by using the leash and collar to direct him slightly.

Photo 4. *The dog must learn to walk on the same side of any obstacle as you do. The pinch collar will hurt if he does not.*

Step 3. *Heeling with distractions in the field.*

This is when you start going through heavy brush; sometimes you are bending over so as to maneuver around a bush or tree, or to crawl under something. It's important that you have someone to help you, someone who will distract the dog's attention by waving his arm, pointing towards something, throwing a stick—whatever you can think of.

After about eight consecutive days of regular training the dog should obey well on the leash *as long as he can feel that the BOSS is concentrating on him.* He will start to make mistakes if he feels that your attention is elsewhere (a little like a kid!). That's why it's so important to maintain your mental concentration on him. It's an important connection that we can use to help our dogs. It's also important that in between exercises you hold the leash correctly. *Only repetition will make the dog respond as if it were a habit.*

You can see now that the leash training is most important, and is the basis for all the following training. I think it is more difficult to teach a hunting dog to heel, than to teach other types of dogs because the hunting dog is so eager to find game. He walks along at heel but his attention can be diverted more easily by what is happening, or he may get a whiff of something interesting, especially if he is in the field. So don't be discouraged with the heeling. It may take a little longer, but it's very important for his future work.

When your dog is fully trained to heel, remind him often by making him heel. If you go out to the end of your driveway to get the mail, take the dog with you and have him heel. It's fun for him because he gets to go out and do something with you, even if it is only for a few minutes. This kind of continued reinforcing helps cement his training for all time.

Chapter Four

The Basic Steps of Force Retrieving

BEFORE BEGINNING THE *retrieving it is absolutely necessary that your dog is completely trained to the Sit, Stay and Heel.* Only then can pressure be used significantly.

Necessary Equipment
1. Short leash and long line
2. Pinch collar
3. Light wooden dummy (See Photo 3.)
4. Stuffed skins of pheasant, quail, duck, etc.
5. Dummy with which you can increase weights.
6. Soft glove (a gardening, or work glove—soft and thick)

No switch is used for the retrieving training.

The Sequence for Force Retrieving:
1. The dog tolerates your hand in his mouth.
2. The dog tolerates the wood dummy and the stuffed skins of birds in his mouth
3. The dog holds a wood dummy and a stuffed bird skin.
4. The dog carries the wood dummy and stuffed bird skins.
5. Repeat step 4 with different dummies.

6. The dog jumps over obstacles with and without dummies.
7. The dog picks up the dummy by himself.
8. The dog grasps the dummy some distance in front of his mouth.
9. The dog picks up a dummy that is lying on the ground.
10. The dog retrieves without help from you.

For all retrieving exercises always be sure that the object (dummy, bird, gloved hand, dead bird) is placed in the dog's mouth carefully so he's comfortable, and the object is not causing pain. A quick and easy solution is to run your bare fingers around his gums, making sure the dummy is not pressing his gums or his tongue down onto his teeth—ouch!

Step 1. *The dog tolerates your hand in his mouth.*

Attach the leash to the dog's collar and have him sit beside your left knee. Then gently drop the leash and take hold of his mouth with your left hand. Using your thumb and middle finger, press against the side of his lips so he opens his mouth. Say "Fetch" and immediately put your gloved right hand, palm up, into his mouth (Photo 1). The backward movement of his head is prevented with your left hand. Keep your hand in the dog's mouth for 10 seconds (count silently to yourself).

Be sure to use a *soft glove* such as a gardening glove. *(The right hand should not be inside the dog's mouth further than ½ to ¾ of an inch behind the canine teeth.)* After a few seconds, say the command "give" or "out" and withdraw your gloved right hand. Encourage the dog with quiet praise. Repeat this step until he tolerates your hand for up to 60 seconds. Increase the time gradually: 10 seconds, 20 seconds, and 30 seconds up to 60. (See Photo 2.)

Limit the training session to only 10 minutes. If you don't succeed in the dog tolerating your hand for 60 seconds within the 10-minute session do it for a length of time that the dog will tolerate, and continue at the next session until the dog will tolerate your gloved hand for 60 seconds.

Photo 1. *The proper way to put your gloved hand into the dog's mouth.*

Photo 2. *The dog holds your gloved hand in his mouth—10 seconds the first time.*

Step 2. *The dog tolerates the wood dummy and other dummies in his mouth.*

Use the same position as in Step 1, but use the wood dummy instead. (See Photo 3.) *Make sure the dummy does not pinch his gums or lips.* When he holds the wood dummy for up to 60 seconds, use the stuffed skins of different birds. This may take up to two days.

Step 3. *The dog holds the dummy and a stuffed bird skin.*

As soon as the dog tolerates the hand, dummy, and stuffed bird, stroke the top of his head gently a few times with soft praise while looking directly into his eyes. (See Photo 3.) Professional trainers know that this makes the dog concentrate on you. *Be alert if the dog attempts to drop the object,* by using your left hand on the collar immediately to stop it, and quickly give the command "fetch."

As training progresses, remove the right hand carefully from the dummy with the command "fetch." (See Photo 4.) Anticipate your dog's every attempt to drop or discard the dummy by quickly using your right hand to stop him, combined with the repeated command "fetch." And remember to always say the command "give" each time you want him to release the dummy into your hand.

Five to twenty repetitions will be necessary to bring the dog to the point where he will hold a dummy or stuffed bird for about one minute. In between these repetitions you should practice the sit and heel. *It is extremely important to have frequent variation to avoid boredom in the dog and to relieve any tension.* Frequent variety requires the dog to pay strict attention, and to concentrate on the Boss.

For example you can have the dog hold the dummy or bird for 60 seconds. Then switch to walking around, heeling for three or four minutes. Then come back to step 3 and continue for 5 more minutes.

Usually three days at the most will be required for the first three steps. Some dogs and some trainers can do it in one day, but whether it takes you one day or three days, or even longer is not important. What is important is to avoid all intimidation. The pressure is quiet, determined and direct, but without great harshness. On the other hand give lavish praise as soon as the dog complies with your wishes.

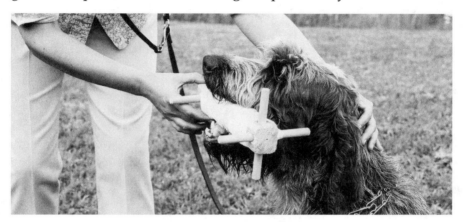

Photo 3. *Place the light wooden dummy into the dog's mouth.*

Photo 4. *The dog holds the dummy while your left hand softly pets him. Your right hand held is held under his chin as a visual aid to prevent him from dropping the dummy.*

For a successful hunting dog it is especially important that *the dog releases or gives the dummy only on the verbal command "give."* Anticipating the give when the dog sees your hand must not become a signal for him to release (give) the dummy. Here is how to avoid sloppy retrieves:

Training for Proper Release of Retrieved Game

As soon as the dog has learned to hold a dummy, we teach him that he must release it only after the command—"give." The dog has excellent sight of motion, which to us makes the training easy. Think back just a moment to how wolves operate to bring down their prey. The pack is moves silently yet communicates to one another through their body language. They don't make a sound but a twitch of an ear is a signal. The pack may be spread out quite far, but the slightest movement is seen by every wolf.

This specific asset of sight that dogs have can work wonders for us as we provide sight clues for the dog. However, in the case of releasing retrieved objects this quality can become a problem. When you take the retrieved object and say "give," the dog quickly connects that the seizure of the dummy is equivalent to the outstretched hand, which is then equivalent to the command "give." The dog opens his mouth prematurely and drops the object.

It's easy to avoid this from the beginning. During the entire training period we use the "give" command only with, or immediately prior to, the seizure of the dummy. Touch the dummy with your right hand, then pull your hand back *without* taking the dummy or saying "give." Repeat this a second time: then the next time say "give," and take the dummy out of the dog's mouth. Keep doing this sequence, changing the number of times you reach with your hand and give no command. This particular step is of great importance for avoiding sloppy retrieving later on. It also forces the dog to concentrate.

To summarize: The dog is sitting with the dummy in his mouth:
Then
1. Pause a few seconds, up to 30 seconds.
2. Stroke the dog's head gently one or two times.
3. Pause a few seconds.
*4. Take hold of the dummy.
5. Pause a few seconds.
6. Pull your hand back.
7. Pause a few seconds.
8. Take hold of the dummy again.
*9. Pause a few seconds.
10. Say the command "give," while taking away the dummy.
11. Praise your dog instantly.

Don't say the command "give" the first time you reach on every retrieve. Dr. Tabel advises, "Do not laugh about these details. The pauses are very important. They train your dog to work correctly." *Steps 4 and 9 above are particularly important. (See General Tips, Chapter 1.)

Remember, do not always command "give" and take hold of the dummy at the same time. Reach toward the dummy, but do not say "give," or take the dummy. Touch the dummy but do not say "give." Do this one time, another time touch it two times, another time three touches. Mix it up. This way the dog will pay strict attention to you and your commands.

Step 4. *The dog carries the light dummy.*

The dog is sitting with the dummy in his mouth. Step in front of him, and take the leash with your left hand just a few inches away from his mouth. Hold your right hand under his mouth. Call the dog by saying "come" and simultaneously step back a few steps. Usually he will try to drop the dummy before he stands up to go to you. Prevent this with your right hand. Use gentle force and encouraging words as you gently but firmly use the leash with a couple of pulls to get him reaching toward you and the dummy. Using the leash puts pressure on the pinch collar which motivates the dog to move toward you, so as soon as he moves let up the pressure on the collar. (See Photo 5.)

If the dog loosens his grip or drops the dummy, do not punish him. Patiently put the dummy in his mouth again and get him to carry it while moving toward you. Ninety percent of the time this step will succeed after 6 to10 repetitions. If not, *be patient;* do not become angry. *Remember that the session should last no more than 10 minutes.* If you can't complete this step on the first day, go back to something he *can do successfully,* and end the session for that day. Be sure *to play with him at the end of the session, and go for a run if possible.* Then do this exercise again the next day.

Once the dog succeeds in taking a few steps toward you while holding the dummy, say "sit" and then say "give." Your voice should be very friendly during this exercise. And once the dog completes this successfully, look into his eyes as you praise him.

You could stop for this day's training here and give your dog praise and a run and then start again the next day. Step Four is a big step; it doesn't have to all be done in one day.

Photo 5. *The first step for the dog to willingly grasp and carry the dummy.*

Step 5. *Repeat step 4 with different dummies (pheasant, duck, chukar, quail, and wood dummies).*

The dog will prefer one or another, but through practice his lack of enthusiasm for a particular dummy or stuffed bird will disappear in a short time.

Sometimes the dog will drop the dummy because he is not carrying it correctly or it might be uncomfortable in his mouth, or, he doesn't want to hold it for a long time. If he drops it say "no" sharply and put the dummy back in his mouth (always making sure his lips and gums aren't being pinched). After several sessions over one-to three days, he should carry the different objects for one to two minutes while walking at heel.

Again, training sessions should be no more than 10 minutes. This prevents the dog from becoming bored and keeps him interested and looking forward to the next training session. Short training sessions also prevents stress for the dog.

Step 6. *Jumping with objects.*

Our dogs like to jump across a ditch or over a low fence. Start with a small ditch, or you can construct a low fence inside your yard. Keep the dog on the leash and walk beside the ditch, or low fence, guiding the dog over it. In the beginning don't use any dummy, just guide him over a few low obstacles. The next time do the same thing but try having him carry a dummy. In this exercise the dog actually pays more attention to the dummy than when he is simply carrying it beside you.

Do this exercise with different dummies out in the field and woods, always on leash. He will do better at home after this bit of training in the fields and woods. Take several days to do this step.

Photo 6. *First lesson in holding the dummy under pressure with the pinch collar.*

Step 7. *The dog grasps the dummy* by himself.

Until now the dog's role has been just to hold the dummy. Now he must do more by grasping (taking hold of) the dummy which is held in front of his mouth. Up to now all the retrieving exercises have not been difficult. This is a difficult step for some dogs, so be patient.

Stand to the right and in front of the sitting dog. The dummy should lie in the palm of your open right hand, your fingertips touching the dog's lower jaw. Your left hand holds his upper jaw as usual. Your command "fetch" causes him to open his mouth as he learned earlier. Move his head a bit forward by using the leash (pressure on the pinch collar), and at the same time lift and tip your right hand so the dummy can roll forward into his open mouth. (You have already done this in step 5, (see photo 5 and 6) but now you will teach the dog to actually move forward to grasp the dummy.

The dog will realize that he can get away from the pressure of the collar only by moving his head forward and grasping the dummy. With every correct movement of the dog—which at first is the spontaneous opening of his mouth—*immediately* stop any pressure on his lips, and any pressure from the leash and pinch collar and *praise him.* Success greatly depends on your ability to quickly recognize the right moment when he obeys the command. You must react according to how he performs. (See photo 7.)

Photo 7. *With just a little pressure from the collar the dog stretches forward to grasp the dummy.*

This first step is difficult, but it's accomplished quickly when the dog has learned that inactivity hurts, and that grasping the dummy stops the pain. *It's wise to stop the training session, after the first successful grasping, with lots of praise for the dog. Repeat this sequence in the next training session, which could be on the same day.* You could plan to have the first session of Step 7 in the morning. That way, if you have success you can have the next session in the evening. If not, it can be done the next day.

After the dog has been successful at grasping the dummy several times, practice the same thing with different dummies and dead birds. Be sure the birds are not frozen. If you remove a frozen bird from your freezer the night before the lesson, it should be completely thawed by the time of the lesson. For training purposes never use a freshly killed, warm bird.

"Never let your dog grasp the dummy through friendly talk or playfulness. Whoever says this about a working hunting dog has no knowledge about this subject." says Dr. Tabel! This is covered in *How To Help Gun Dogs Train Themselves.* Never play with a young dog by throwing a dummy for him, or throwing anything in play. Retrieving is a serious job for the dog. We play with our dogs, but not with dummies or birds. And your family must understand this, especially the kids.

"Force will be increased now. At this stage the dog should not grasp the dummy because he enjoys it, but because he has to. Only then can we successfully go back later to our first steps in case of possible mistakes." Dr. Tabel.

Step 8. *The dog grasps the dummy farther away from his mouth.*

When the dog has grasped the dummy about 12 times, gradually move the dummy farther away from his mouth while you hold the dummy by one end. At first the distance between the dummy and the dog's mouth is only a few inches; it will be increased very gradually up to three feet. The left hand holds the leash and guides the dog to the dummy. He does not approach it by himself (See Photo 8). Again, it's very important that at the right moment you change quickly from force to praise.

Photo 8. *The dog picks up the dummy from the ground while you continue to hold one end of the dummy with your right hand.*

As you increase the distance between dummy and mouth, also gradually lower the dummy until it nearly touches the ground. It's possible that several dozen repetitions of these exercises will be needed before the dog consistently goes forward on the command "fetch" and grasps the dummy. When he hesitates, remind him by using the pinch collar and leash. (See Photo 7.) After each grasping the dummy (with much praise), the dog should carry it for a few moments while heeling and then be made to sit, waiting for the command "give" before releasing it.

Sometimes the dog will do well but then suddenly refuse to go forward and grasp the dummy. In this case do not show any agitation, and do not intimidate senselessly by yelling, jerking on the collar or hitting the dog. If you don't achieve success after several tries with a reasonable use of the pinch collar, return to the previous exercise. You may have advanced too quickly.

Step 8 should take place over several days, perhaps even a week. *When this step is done satisfactorily 8 to 10 times with various light weight dummies, go on to Step 9.*

Step 9. *The dog picks up the dummy from the ground.*

Keep doing Step 8 but gradually lower the dummy so that the dog is grasping it close to the ground. After the dog repeatedly grasps the dummy close to the ground put one end of the dummy on the ground while you keep the other end in your hand. (See Photo 8.) If he does well, the next time touch the dummy lightly and finally not at all. Instead your pointing finger becomes a visual aid for the dog. Bend over and point a few inches from the dummy.

This step, moving from grasping the dummy from your hand to picking up the dummy up from the ground gives some dogs difficulty. To make it easier, lay the dummy on two bricks on edge which are 12 inches apart. After this is successful, turn the bricks flat with the dummy resting on both bricks. After this is successful, lay the dummy on the ground between the bricks. (See photos 10, 11, 12.)

The first time you use the bricks use your visual aid by pointing your finger just a few inches from the dummy.

Twenty to thirty repeats are necessary until the dog attains a fairly steady performance. Of course, he will not always go to the dummy and grasp it. Often you must help by using the collar and leash. This is good! He is learning that he has to do the exercise because you want it and not because it's fun for him.

When he does this exercise with the light dummy; repeat it with a bird, duck, or heavier dummy (in preparation for retrieving a large goose).

Photo 10. *Place the dummy on each end of the raised bricks and lead the dog toward the dummy, giving the fetch command.*

Photo 11. *Repeat with the bricks laid down.*

Photo 12. *This time the dummy is lying on the ground between the bricks.*

Step 10. *"Fetch," the dog goes for the dummy.*

Until now you always stood beside the dummy. Often you had to use the leash and collar to help the dog. Now he must learn to go alone to the dummy, pick it up, and bring it back to you.

The dog sits leashed as usual beside you. Throw the dummy a few steps ahead so he sees where it falls. Be sure he remains sitting. After a short pause, take a step with your left leg in the direction of the dummy, and at the same time give the command "fetch." While the dog is picking up the dummy immediately step back a step or two and encourage him with much praise. Be sure he sits when he returns. Then command "give," and take the dummy away from him while praising him. After several repetitions, shorten your "escort" and only pretend a forward movement. Finally, make no movement at all.

When the dog has learned this step well, change from the short leash to a long leash and let him bring you different objects from 7 to 12 yards away. Now he will usually show that he enjoys working, even more so if you occasionally have him jumping over some barriers or a low fence while he is retrieving.

Remember, if the dog is not performing correctly, go back and do the last step that he did perfectly. Then go forward in the training, with lots of praise.

Now move this work to the fields and woods, away from his normal training place. The ice is broken!

CHAPTER FIVE

Retrieving In the Field and Water

THE SECOND PART of retrieving training takes place mostly in the field, away from home. One aspect of this part is building and refining what the dog has already learned, but now doing it in the field away from home. It also gives the dog a chance to learn to do more difficult aspects of what he already knows, like retrieving a heavy piece of game (say a goose for example) from a long distance.

Another part of this training is *teaching the dog to do some of his work away from his Boss, and in some cases, out of sight of his Boss.* This work prepares him for future hunting when wounded game may have escaped and perhaps moved into the woods, or across a pond and into the brush. In these situations where the dog is out of your sight and you are out of his sight, the dog has to be well balanced in his own self confidence and in his desire to please you in order to do his work. He will develop this balance as he goes through the training and in actually doing the work. Your dog will enjoy the field training even more than in the yard!

Step 1. *Preparing the dog to retrieve from your back track.*

When you walk through the woods or across a field with the dog on leash, the track you both leave is called a back track.

Put the dog on the long leash. Walk to a larger training area, such as your front lawn, or nearby field, park (with no distractions), or empty school yard. While walking drop or toss the dummy along the way so he sees the dummy fall. Continue walking for five steps. Stop, and as soon as the dog sits give him the command "fetch" and immediately point toward the dropped dummy. Usually he will go immediately to the dropped dummy, pick it up, and bring it back to you because he is used to doing it. He is still on the long leash so you need to play out the leash so that he can reach the dummy. Make sure he completes the retrieve properly; sitting and holding the dummy until you say "give."

Go back with him a few steps if necessary. After two or three repetitions, increase the distance to 10, 15, 18 yards. Finally, if he has retrieved confidently and joyfully, work him without the leash, first 5 yards, then 10, 15, 18.

Throughout this exercise be very alert that the long line doesn't tangle the dog. At the same time use this opportunity to condition him to the presence of the long line in preparation for the beginning training of retrieving from water later in this chapter. When he is not actually doing a task, perhaps sitting next to you, or standing beside you, casually run the leash lightly up and down his leg. Another time casually let it lay across his back. If the line disturbs him at all, try petting him and reassuring him with your voice.

Do not rush working without the leash. The leash is our best tool to show the dog that his Boss always has control, that his Boss is omnipotent. As long as the dog still tries to disobey an order, as long as he still needs help, *under no circumstances should you take him off the leash* during exercises outside the fenced yard or training area. If he obeys your commands on the long leash repeatedly, trustfully and with joy (wagging his tail, etc.), you can work him off the leash without any doubts. *Start with short distances first, gradually increasing the distance. Don't rush it!*

Step 2. *Retrieving the dummy from the back track and teaching the dog to retrieve at full speed.*

The best way to get your dog to be a joyful retriever, in addition to his jumping over fences and ditches, is to retrieve the dummy from the back track. Dogs like to do this—for them it's fun. And it's the best way to teach your dog to retrieve quickly.

Do this work on a dirt road, or wide path in the woods, or along the edge of a field, but drop the dummy so that the dog *does not see it*. As you walk down a two track, path, or lane, or trail with him working ahead of you, carefully drop the dummy just beyond the edge of the trail, so that the dog can't see it. Don't put it more than one yard from the trail because you want him to use his nose on the track to find the bird.

Continue to walk for 20 to 25 yards. Stop and give your dog the command "fetch" and use your arm signal—raised arm pointing in the direction of the object to be retrieved. Usually he will run back 12 to 18 yards because he already knows to run back that far. He should then use his nose to find the dummy. When he sees it he will hurry to it, pick it up and retrieve it to you.

If necessary, go back with him and repeat the command "fetch" with great enthusiasm and encouragement. Usually no more than six to eight repetitions are needed to get him to understand. From now on he will run back (on the back track) to search for the dummy. He is learning to find the dummy by using his memory, his eyes, and his nose to follow your footsteps and his own tracks.

As soon as the dog reaches the dummy and picks it up, go forward (away) from the dog as fast as possible. Running is best or even fast walking. The dog tries very hard to reach you and will arrive at full speed. Make sure he sits and holds the dummy until you give the command to "give." Soon it will become a habit for him to retrieve as fast as he can. As you increase the distance he will hurry even more. Gradually increase the distance to 50, 60, 100 yards and more.

It is not hard to get your dog to follow your back track for miles. Your foot-prints, and his, leave a heavy scent. Sometimes you can step off the path and walk several yards into woods. This teaches him to pay attention to the scent of the back track and not to depend entirely on his eyes and memory. He is learning *concentration on the track and how to use his nose*, vital attributes for a successful hunting dog in recovering wounded game.

During all of Step 2 remember to change the dummies often, using the different stuffed bird skins and later use heavier dummies.

Retrieving from the back track is very important for future training so don't treat it lightly. You are laying a base for having a dog that will never fail to bring you wounded or dead game.

Red Alert! Do not do the retrieve from a back track *more than two times* on an outing. Some days *do only one,* other days do two. *Some days avoid doing any.*

Stop a training session when the dog still wants to do more, not when he is tired or bored.

Step 3. *Fetch. The dog brings light and heavy objects up to a 20 pound dummy.*

This step gives the dog experience in retrieving objects of different weights. It also builds the muscles necessary for retrieving heavy pieces of game such as geese.

The dog learns from the experience of retrieving various objects. Now you must vary the training a bit so he learns to adjust the manner and strength of his grip. A 15-pound dummy requires a different grip from retrieving a quail or pheasant. He must develop his muscular system and his technique for carrying heavier items.

An excellent method for teaching the correct grip is for the dog to retrieve heavy objects over obstacles—ditches, streams, fallen trees, up and down hills, through thick brush. He does this on your back track, so from time to time you must leave a back track with a heavier dummy. However, when your dog has advanced to a heavy object he should only retrieve a heavy object over a log or ditch once a day, to avoid overtaxing a young dog.

Sometimes when the dog is retrieving a heavy dummy over an obstacle, the dummy or bird falls out of his mouth when he lands on the ground. Watch this and teach him to pick it up by himself immediately. He will do it more easily when you don't stand right beside the obstacle. If the dummy falls out of the dog's mouth and you see that the dog intends to pick it up, quickly move 5 to 15 steps backward, away from him. *This builds a sense of urgency in the dog to reach you as quickly as he can with the object.*

Continue this training until the large dog can carry 15 pounds for five minutes (the small dog 10 pounds) without getting seriously tired. This is the only way can you increase his capacity for work; later he will not refuse to retrieve heavy game.

Retrieving from Water

When the dog has thoroughly learned the steps for retrieving on land, including retrieving from the back track and over obstacles, the transition to retrieving objects from shallow, and then deep water is an easy task. *Don't rush the water work until the dog is completely reliable on land.*

This book assumes that you conditioned your dog to water when he was much younger and now is absolutely comfortable in water. If he is not, do not attempt the retrieving from water training until he is 100 percent comfortable swimming in deep water and has experienced his first hunting season.

It is best to find *a small pond with very gradual depth change*, including some water that is not swimming depth. (See photo 1.) This means the *entry into the water is very gradual.* Such a setting gives the dog more confidence than a huge lake or a steep drop off as soon as he hits water.

Make sure his *first water retrieving work is not done in cold water.* If it is late fall, winter, or early spring, wait for warmer water. You can continue with the rest of the training: drop, drag track, etc. When the water is warm start the water retrieving.

Photo 1. *This is an ideal depth for early work in retrieving from water. The dog's feet are just touching the bottom of the pond. (Compliments Rem DeJong.)*

Step 1. *Retrieving dummy from water at a distance of six to eight feet.*

Be sure there are no distractions—other dogs, other people or wild ducks.

The dog wears the training collar and the long line is attached. Have your dog at the "sit" about 6 feet from the edge of the water. Wade into the shallow water 6 to 8 feet and lay the dummy in the water so that the dog can easily watch you put the dummy into the water. Return to the dog. Stand so that the dog is on your left side as usual. Give the command to fetch, point toward the dummy, and take one step forward with your left foot, while feeding out the line as he moves toward the dummy, being careful not to tangle the dog in the line.

Stand at the edge of the water for this early water retrieving training. After he picks up the dummy and heads for shore, remember that as soon as he reaches shore he will want to put the dummy down to shake off the water. Prevent this by watching closely. If he starts to let go of the bird repeat "fetch." If necessary repeat the "fetch" yet again.

When he was a young dog and you were conditioning him to retrieve from water, you met him at the edge of the water to prevent him from putting the duck down to shake. He's older now and must learn that he must hold the duck until you tell him to give. Gradually, as he succeeds in his water retrieves, move back from the shore line. Do it one step at a time, that is, one successful retrieve at a time, until you are 10 or 12 feet from shore and the dog is bringing the game all the way to you, and waiting for your command to "give."

If he drops the dummy immediately go to him and put the dummy back in his mouth, while giving him the fetch command again. Then walk backward to where you and the dog were, allowing the dog to complete the retrieve.

When this is successful move on to step 2. But if this first step is at all sloppy do it again and work for improvement. It may take three tries before he is successful. Step 1 may be done over the course of two to three days if necessary.

The distance for the first water retrieves, with the dog on the long line, should be only 8 or 10 feet. Gradually work up to 20 feet, no longer than that.

Step 2. *Retrieving different objects.*

Continue with Step 1, but use a variety of objects for the dog to retrieve: different dummies, dead birds, especially a dead duck. Using different kinds of birds keeps it more interesting for the dog. Be sure all dead birds are completely thawed. Do this for two lessons. If the dog is successful in retrieving all the different objects with clean retrieves, no dropping the bird, etc., then go on to the next step. *Make sure the dog doesn't get tangled in the long line.*

Step 3. *Retrieving dummies and dead birds for longer distances.*

After success with Steps 1 and 2, throw the dummy out into the water so it is twice as far and in swimming depth water, but *no farther than 20 feet because of the danger of the dog becoming tangled in the long line.* Have the dog retrieve it to you as above. Make sure the retrieve is done correctly including not setting the dummy or bird down at the edge of the water to shake. Again, be alert so that the dog doesn't get tangled in the long line.

Step 4. *Retrieving off the line.*

After two or three successful retrieves as in Step 3, begin retrieving without the long line. The dog sits beside your left knee. Make sure he remains sitting. Walk into the water about six or eight feet and lay the dummy in the water. Go back to the dog, quietly unsnap the long line and give the "fetch" command. *Meet him as he is returns to shore and make sure he does not lay the dummy down at the edge of the water.* When he brings the dummy don't forget the instant praise. Good Boy!

The first time that you do Step 4, stop after 2 successful retrieves. Too many retrieves during a training session can easily sour a dog. Stop while he still wants to do more work! Vary your training sessions. Work on other training things and about every other day do more retrieving, both on land and from water, to build up his confidence, and his experience.

All further water retrieving training should be done without a collar or line to avoid the dog becoming tangled in anything.

CHAPTER SIX

Chasing a Duck: Building Desire

THIS EXERCISE DOES many things for the young dog that hasn't had a lot of hunting experience, and even for those who have had a hunting season but little waterfowl work. It builds his inborn desire for game contact. It is that desire, that drive that makes the best gun dog. A really good gun dog should want to find game more than anything else in life. Chasing a duck helps an inexperienced dog build that desire.

Do not attempt this unless your dog is very comfortable swimming in deep water. He should enjoy entering water, enjoy swimming around and shows no fear of water.

Chasing a duck is described in *How To Help Gun Dogs Train Themselves* (pp. 157-160) as a means to condition young dogs to become comfortable in the water. You can use many of the same procedures now.

Finding Good Water

Find a small pond. Reeds and cover around some of the edges are okay. It should have a very gradual entry; if it's not swimming depth that's also okay. You don't want to do this in extremely cold weather, so a fall day that isn't too cold is fine, or the middle of the spring, and of course summer is fine.

Finding and Caring for Ducks

Find someone who raises mallards for training purposes. You'll find lists of game bird farms online and elsewhere and in the Appendix; word of mouth is often a great and best source. Once you find a resource, you'll need a proper cage to carry them home. Once home set the crate in a few inches of water until you can use them. Keep the ducks well fed and watered if they are not sitting in water.

You can use a small plastic tarp placed in a small depression which you can fill with water. This will make a puddle big enough for you to set the duck cage at the edge of the depression so drinking water is available for the ducks at all times. (Note: See below for suggestions regarding treatment of game birds used for training.)

Make arrangements so that you can pick up the ducks just a day or two before you plan to do this piece of training. That way the ducks will be fresh and will work a lot better than if they are kept in a crate for several days.

Caution for the care and use of birds for training

Although you have been using a few thawed dead birds from your freezer, now you will be using live birds. Caution is advised that you do this out of sight of the public as much as possible. There is enough anti-hunting being spread around; we don't want to add to that. When you expect to use live birds, especially the ducks for training, do it in an out-of-the-way place where you won't expect the public wandering past. And don't talk to people about this part of the training, except for other hunters.

The same advice when you are using a pheasant, or chukar, with the feathers pulled from one wing. When non hunters see this activity it doesn't do our cause any good. Be discrete when using live birds for training.

Don't leave dead birds used for training lying around any where. Always pack them out.

Photos 1 and 2. *Above and below you can see how this young dog is building his desire for game! He's intense and focused 100 percent on getting the duck! (Photos by the author.)*

First outing with a duck

For the first lesson it is extremely important to have a friend and his dog join you. The dog should be well trained and experienced in retrieving ducks from the water. A third person to help will make things go more smoothly. Instruct your friend ahead of time as to what you need from him. If you don't have someone with a trained dog available you can still do this but it will require more time and more sessions to have the same successful outcome.

Make a duck flightless by taping down both wings. The duck will not be able to fly. It will be able to swim but not well. For the very first time tape the duck so that it can't swim very fast because you want your young dog to be able to catch the duck fairly easily.

Instruct the third person ahead of time as to what you want him to do. At the first session you and your dog, and your friend with his dog, should stand near the water's edge—you standing, the dog sitting by your left knee, the other dog and his owner as well. The helper holds the duck and *while the dogs are watching the helper wades in a foot or two and releases the duck.* He waves his arms, claps his hands, to get the duck to move away a bit.

The dogs will probably start whining and perhaps yipping at this point. It's okay for now, because they should want to go. With the duck not able to swim very well it makes it easy for the dogs to catch it so they can be successful. In a real hunting situation you want your dog to be silent at the blind (See Chapter 9, Steady At The Blind.). The primary aim now is to build desire for game in your young dog, especially waterfowl and working in water. It's okay if he whines and yips during this lesson. Later he will learn to be quiet at the blind, even when ducks are gliding into the decoys.

As soon as the helper gets out of the water, your friend with the older, experienced retriever should send his dog to get the duck. Your dog should be very excited now, probably yipping and barking and crying. That's good. You just stay calm. *As soon as the other dog delivers the duck to your friend, both you and your friend should lavish praise on his dog.*

Now your friend's dog should do another retrieve. The helper places the duck a little farther out and the older dog makes another retrieve. Again, both of you pour on the praise for that dog.

Your friend now puts his dog on leash. The helper carries the duck into the water again, but closer to shore. As soon as he releases the duck and gets out of the way, encourage your dog to "fetch!" Your dog should swim fast and grab the duck, turn and start swimming toward shore. Stand near the edge of the water so that you can prevent him from putting the duck down to shake. By standing at the edge you are supporting the dog a little more than in the past retrieving exercises, but only until he builds his desire for working in the water. Soon you will stand farther back and require him to bring the duck all the way to you.

If the first retrieve is successful, do another one with the duck placed just one yard further out. Have your friend and his dog stay where he is so the feeling of competition between the two dogs is still there, acting as an incentive for the younger dog. After the successful retrieve, quit for the day.

The next day do some training in the field. The following day, or two days later, go back to the water with your friend and his dog. Do everything again, but increase the distances a little.

After a week or two, try this without your friend and his dog. If your dog doesn't show as much desire to get the duck as he did when the other dog was there, then get the other dog back again. If your dog is not really excited about the water work, go back to the field work for a few days or a week. Then come back to the water and have the other dog there too. The other dog promotes competition and helps the younger, less experienced dog build up his desire for game.

As long as this particular water exercise remains successful, and the dog is happy with the experience, you can come back once in a while. It's important that you find a different pond to continue this work so that your dog will experience water retrieving at different places, and he learns that he has to retrieve *wherever* and *whenever* you command him to do so.

Depending on when your dog was born he may not be ready to do this water work in the spring, or in the fall. That's okay, you can go on to the next chapter and when the weather warms you can come back with your friend and his dog and do this work. Working with flightless ducks is good preparation for future duck hunting and additional water retrieving training (See Chapter 10).

Using an upland bird prior to the duck work

If you want to work on building more desire in your dog before he chases a duck, or if he hasn't experienced a hunting season yet, you can use a flightless pheasant. Use a hen so there is no risk of your dog getting spurred. After removing eight wing feathers from one wing (which makes the bird unable to fly), your helper releases the bird so the dog can watch the bird run away. Do this where cover is short so your dog can see the bird running away. Once the bird has gone 20 yards, release your dog. Let him chase and track the bird, catch it and bring it to you. This exercise always gets the young dog excited and builds desire. Do this no more than two times. (For this work get pheasants that are good runners; birds that haven't been cooped up in a crate for a long time.) Start working on chasing the duck at the next field outing.

The water work is how we teach our dogs to recover wounded ducks, and at the same time build up the dog's desire for game, their enthusiasm to *get the bird!* This also helps in conditioning the dog physically. Swimming and searching in swimming-depth water is hard work, and provides the opportunity for him to learn a little about ducks so he will become an efficient retriever of wounded ducks and other game.

Dr. Tabel's General Overall Retrieving Training Tips

1. If your dog shows an undecided, faint-hearted manner while retrieving a bird and other game, *do not go toward him.* Instead walk backwards a few steps, while encouraging and praising him with great enthusiasm.

2. Some dogs—usually those who enjoy retrieving very much— circle their Boss while holding the piece of game and wagging their tails proudly. They forget to immediately sit down. This is not a big fault in itself, but don't allow the dog to let this become a habit. Get him used to a quick "sit" with a light tap on his rump. Do not praise a dog that likes to show his joy *before* he delivers the game.

3. Give special attention when he retrieves a duck or goose from deep water. He will often stop when he gets to the shore, drop the duck, and shake. In a hunting situation the duck is occasionally still alive and could get away when the dog sets it down to shake. The moment the dog touches the shore the Boss should quickly take several steps *backwards*. It's wrong to go toward the dog or to punish him verbally. *This advice is for the trained dog who understands what's expected of him.*

Photos 3&4. *The reason we want our dogs to retrieve whatever we shoot is here in these photos: Above our cover girl, SORA, with a chukar on an early winter hunt. (Compliments Joe Schmutz.) Below: an early snow in Nebraska produces a duck off a creek bottom. (Author and her dog.)*

CHAPTER SEVEN

Drop—
The Ultimate Command

THE "DROP" IS t*he best method for gaining complete control of your hunting dog at all times.* This command provides much more control than the conventional "whoa," or "down." When your dog is fully trained to the "drop," you will be able to stop him with one command from the whistle even when he is 150 yards away. Dr. Tabel considered the "drop" to be the most important command for training a hunting dog. Without this you will never have full control of your dog at all times.

In Dr. Tabel's book, the command in the German language is "Halt!" When you look up halt in an English dictionary it says, as a verb, "to bring to a halt; a military order to stop." When we did the original translation the best word we could come up with, other than using halt, was "drop." Henry, Dr. Tabel's son, agreed that "drop" came as close as we could get to the original.

Do not begin this training until your dog is fully trained in the "sit," " stay," and " heel," and all the retrieving training in Chapters 4 and 5, including the retrieve from your back track (in Chapter 4).

Equipment Needed: You already have all of this equipment which you used in Chapters 2, 3, 4 and 5:

1. **Two-tone whistle** from Germany, with the higher-pitched sound at the thin end (for "come") and the stronger, louder triller at the thicker end for the long blast to command "drop."

2. **Short, over-the-shoulder leash.**

3. **Long leash or line**, 20-30 feet.

4. **Pinch Collar** (pinch collar that you have been using up to now).

5. **Small switch** (as used before in the early sit training).

Step 1. *Use the short leash and have your dog sitting at your left knee.*

Put the leash down and put your left hand over the dog's neck and over the pinch collar. Say "drop" and at the same time use your right hand to simultaneously lift and pull his front legs out in front of him while pushing him down with your left hand, thus forcing him to lie down. (See Photo 1.) The dog's head must be pressed all the way to the ground between his front legs. If your dog is at all "soft," or timid, press only on the neck with no pressure on the collar.

The dog will usually try to rise the first time. Stop this rise with your left hand spread over his back at the kidney region, putting pressure there. Keep the dog in this position for 30 to 40 seconds with *very slight, quiet praise* ("good boy") once or twice. (See Photo 2.) This is the proper "drop" position. It isn't terribly important to have the absolutely correct position the first time, but it is important his head is kept on the ground, or on his front legs, not raised. He must learn and understand that he is not punished as long as he remains in the "drop" position. If he attempts to raise his head or rise, he will feel the collar spikes pressing into his neck

After 30-40 seconds give the command "come," which allows the dog to stand. Then say "heel" and walk around a bit before practicing the lesson one more time, or go to Step 2.

Photo 1. *Put your left hand on the pinch collar; give the command "drop" and push the dog to the ground while the right hand lifts the dog's front legs out from under him.*

Photo 2. *Hold the dog in the drop position some 30 to 40 seconds, with very slight praise (once or twice a quiet "good boy").*

Step 2. *The dog stays in the drop while you stand up.*

As soon as the dog no longer tries to raise his head, roll over, or get up, gradually lift your hands. (See Photo 3.) If he attempts to raise his head, immediately press on the pinch collar, while pressing the head down and say "drop." Repeat as long as necessary until he lies quietly when you take your hands away.

Gradually stand erect beside the lying dog for *up to one minute.* Have your switch in one hand above his head, making sure the dog will be punished every time he attempts to raise his head. If he raises his head at all quickly tap the top of his head lightly with the switch (but enough to feel uncomfortable). (See Photo 4.)

Always release the dog from this position by saying "Come" and short praise—a quiet, brisk "Good boy." Then lead him away with the command "heel."

Usually it takes no more than 20 to 30 repetitions over the course of 2 to 3 days until the dog understands that when he hears "drop" he has to lie down with his head close to the ground between his front feet, or resting on his feet.

Remember the lesson should be no longer than 10 minutes. Don't forget at the end of the lesson as soon as you release him from a command, play with your dog a bit immediately and if at all possible take him for a run, even if it's only for 10 minutes. In between the steps of "drop," walk the dog around a minute at heel. This breaks the tension for the dog and makes him feel a little better about himself and about you.

Photo 3. *Gradually lift your hands and stand erect.*

Photo 4. *Stand beside the dog with the switch in one hand held above the dog's head. Tap him on the head if he attempts to raise his head.*

Step 3. *Teaching the dog to go down into the drop without pulling his front legs out, and learning the new visual signal of your raised arm.*

The dog sits beside you with the switch close at hand. Put the end of the leash straight down from the dog's neck under your left foot while you hold the leash tightly with your free hand. Give the command "drop" and lift your right arm vertically. At the same time use your other hand to give the leash a sharp tug down. This move will pull his front part to the ground. If he tries to get up, immediately use the switch on top of his head---not too hard but a tap that's enough to be uncomfortable. We have to teach the dog to go down in a flash.

From now on pay attention to his correct position. He should lie straight on his hind legs, his front legs stretched forward completely and his head flat on the ground between his feet. All these details are important. Of primary importance is always pressing his head to the ground very quickly whenever he attempts to raise it. The reason the dog hates to go into the full drop (head on the ground between his feet) is because that is a very submissive behavior and canines do not want to feel or appear submissive. This is an important psychological edge for you.

Later, when you are in the woods or fields and your voice isn't loud enough, you will use the whistle (the long trill on the thick end of the whistle). The dog learns the meaning of the whistle in two days at the most as follows: When he learns to drop when you raise your arm (see Photo 5) you do not have to say "Drop." Instead blow the whistle. This is fairly easy for the dog to learn. Making the transition to the whistle he will see the familiar raised arm and then hear the whistle, but no voice command.

After three or four repetitions, *if the dog is careless in dropping quickly simultaneously use the whistle and the switch. This combination will make the dog understand.* This exercise must be repeated again and again until it becomes a solid, consistent habit for the dog. It is now most important to repeat the "Drop" exercise uncounted times correctly, using the three different commands: the whistle, the raised arm, and the voice. *This is the basis for all future training.*

Photo 5. *When the dog has learned "drop"for the raised arm, do not say the command; instead blow the whistle---a single blast on the triller end (the thick end).*

Photo 6. *From behind the dog, hold the switch over the dog's nose.*

Step 4. *The dog stays in the drop while you walk around him.*

Have your dog in the drop position, head flat on the ground between his front feet. Take the leash in your left hand, the switch in your right hand. Hold the switch threateningly above the dog's head and move forward then take two steps backward in front of the dog, then to his left side, then to his right side. If he stays in this position go behind him. He will probably try to turn his head so he can still see you. Hold the switch from behind, over his nose. The dog will keep his head to the ground because he knows what the switch means. (See Photo 6.)

Gradually increase the distance from the dog, go around him, step over him, poke him with the switch, get some distractions from a helper such as throwing a ball so the dog can see with his head on the ground, or have someone calling. (See Photos 7 and 8.)

The dog is still on the leash all the time. Keep increasing the distance between you and him. As you increase the distance, change to the long leash. Every time he attempts to get up, give a sharp jerk downward on the pinch collar and repeat the command "drop." Gradually increase the time he must remain in the "drop" up to at least 5 minutes, even if you are out of sight or when there are disturbances. You'll probably need a helper, someone to cause disturbances, perhaps hiding in some woods and making some noises. If *you* are out of sight making a noise, the helper must enforce the command.

This step will take, perhaps, up to seven days. Remember, only 10 minutes of training per session, followed by some play. Mix other training he already knows in between—walk at heel, retrieving from land and water.

Later, sometimes in actual hunting conditions, the dog will have to remain stationary for a much longer time. After the training is finished it's important that he always drops quickly every time. The correct drop position won't be necessary at that time, but for now it is.

Photo 7. *Walk over the dog a few times, insisting that he keep his head flat on the ground between his front legs. Press his head down if necessary.*

Photo 8. *Use all kinds of distractions—poking him gently with the switch, throwing a bone out ahead of him, making noises. The dog must stay in the drop position despite all disturbances and distractions.*

Step 5. *The dog drops from the standing position, then while walking and jogging.*

When the dog has thoroughly mastered steps 1 to 4, begin training him to drop from the standing position (as opposed to sitting). Have the dog walk at heel and drop. Next jog with the dog at heel and have him drop from what would probably be a fast trot for him. Now keep changing your speed so that the dog learns he must drop from *any* speed. Do a fast walk, a trot, running as fast as you can, and vary it each time so he learns to pay close attention to your speed.

When the dog is dropping at any speed without problems, or without hesitation, do the exercise at a run, blow the whistle for the drop command *while you keep running*. The dog drops while you run on.

There should be little difficulty with this exercise, especially if you immediately correct him if he hesitates at all. Correct quickly with the switch and collar. Don't allow any hesitation.

Step 6. *"Drop" at various distances from the trainer and with distractions.*

When the dog drops quickly on command—verbally, with whistle, and with the raised hand and when he also comes immediately on "come," or with two peeps on the whistle, start doing the drop at a distance from you.

Have the dog sitting, standing or walking in the yard on the long leash at a distance of two to three yards from you. At a moment when he doesn't expect a command, give the command "drop" by lifting your right arm vertically. Usually he will drop promptly. If he hesitates, jerk the leash downward and use the switch. Be sure he is in the correct position—with his head on the ground between his front feet.

Gradually increase the distance until you have used the entire length of the line, so the dog is 20-30 feet from you. Have the dog drop at 7 feet, then 9, and so on until he is dropping 20-30 feet from you. *Remember that whenever you want the dog to get up from the drop you must go to him and give a command to release him—come or heel. Never call him to you.* If you begin calling him to you, he may begin to anticipate leaving from the drop.

Only when he is fully trained to the drop *can you have him drop in the field and then call him to you, but only then.* Even when he is fully trained, sometimes give the drop command and walk to him to release him instead of calling him to you. This re-enforces the drop and maintains the well trained dog.

Step 7. *Drop outside the yard.*

Once dropping in the yard is successful, move outside the yard, perhaps to your front yard, an empty school yard, or a vacant lot nearby. It must be away from the "training yard." So you may have to go by car to find a suitable place. But it must be away from the "training yard." Not only will you be in a different place, but also there will not be a fence and there will be *distractions.*

Initially, practice as you have. Practicing outside the yard will be a new situation for the dog so begin with something he already knows a couple of times to give him confidence in the new surroundings. Practice as in previous steps. Have the dog drop a couple of times, first at 5 yards and a second time at 10 yards.

As soon as the dog seems comfortable with the new surroundings, begin adding distractions. You may want to wait until the second visit to the new place. For example, you can have him at the drop and have a helper toss a bone, or dummy so that he sees it. If he starts to move out of the drop position, even a lifting of his head to watch, be quick to correct the dog back into the proper position. It may be that all you need to do is give the command once. Verbal is probably the best and fastest way at this point.

Do all kinds of different things: perhaps have the dog walk at heel along your sidewalk and give the command to drop. Do this in various new situations when he doesn't expect the drop command.

Transition from Dropping When You are Beside the Dog to Not Being Beside Him When He Drops

Step 8. *The dog learns to drop when you are not beside him.*

Your helper should be someone the dog knows well so he is comfortable, at ease, and confident. The helper should run with the dog at heel on the leash, while you remain stationary. Blow the whistle for the drop, the long triller sound. If the dog hesitates to drop your helper must immediately make him drop. *The helper must know and understand exactly how to do this, so it's up to you to instruct him well before the lesson.*

Always watch for the dog's correct and quick execution of commands. Carelessness should be punished swiftly, but praise should be lively when he does well. He will come to understand that the "drop" position doesn't mean unpleasantness for him, and once this part of the training is completed the rest goes quite easily.

Do not hurry through these exercises. Each step should be done only when the previous steps have been accomplished well. Finally, work on the drop in the fields and woods until the dog drops quickly at distances up to 150 yards. Of utmost importance is that *the dog must go down when commanded. Slackness or hesitation should not be tolerated under any condition.*

Whatever lesson you are teaching your dog, every training session should end with success and then with a playful romp and praise for the dog. If you can take the dog for a short run after the lesson, or even a ride to the store, anything that he enjoys doing *with you* is good. This helps cement the relationship between you and the dog.

After some months and a lot of experience in the field—every dog is different— eventually the dog does not have to go down on the ground for the drop. Gradually, especially out in the field, whether hunting or not, when you blow the drop command *the dog will stop dead in his tracks and hold that.* And that will be sufficient. But that comes a lot later when you have full confidence that he will always stop on the drop command. In your daily life keep re-enforcing the "drop" as well as all the other things your dog has learned even when he is older. Insist that he go all the way down once in a while.

Remember the dog does not like to go into the full drop because of the submissive position. It makes him feel uncomfortable. So it's good to make him do it once in a while so you always have the upper hand, that extra edge.

.

CHAPTER EIGHT

Retrieving from a Drag Track

A DRAG TRACK IS a track that is laid by dragging a cold (not frozen) dead piece of game 150 yards ending out of the dog's sight. It is quite different from retrieving from a back track, but the work on the back track prepares the dog for the drag track. Also, it's easier to train your dog to retrieve from a drag track if he is already trained to the drop, because with the drop you have great control over the dog even if he is 100 yards from you.

To lay a drag track tie a lightweight piece of rope or string around a dead piece of game. It should not be a warm, freshly killed bird. (You should have dead birds in your freezer to use for training. Take the frozen bird out of your freezer the night before training.) Drag it along the ground for about 100 or 150 yards, ending in woods or brush so that when the dog reaches the dead game he is out of sight of the Boss. Untie the string and go hide down wind. That's how you lay a drag track for a dog that is fully trained to do it.

Step 1. *First drag track.*

You will need a helper for this training. Put the pinch collar on the dog and attach the long line. Have the dog sit beside the helper by his left knee. The helper holds the leash and lets the dog watch you drag the dead bird eight yards or so. Remove the string and walk back to the dog parallel and downwind of the track a few yards away, being careful not to walk on the track. When you reach the dog take hold of the collar, unsnap the leash, point toward the spot where the drag started and tell him to "fetch." (*See below for correct way to send the dog on the track.) Be sure to play out the line so he can reach the game.

Do several of these short, successful drags using the long line, but no more than three at this time. *Be sure to insist on a proper retrieve.* Correct this if necessary.

Step 2. *First drag off the long line.*

Step 2 should be done the following day while the first lesson is still fresh in the dog's mind. Start by doing one retrieve with the dog on the long line, just as in Step 1. If he is successful in the retrieve on the long line, start step 2 with the dog sitting beside the helper so the dog can watch you lay the track. This time drag the dead bird about six yards, then turn off the path into woods or brush and go a short distance (no more than two to three yards) out of sight of the dog. Be sure the place you stop in the woods is fairly open so he will find the bird easily. Untie the string and leave the game and return to the dog, being careful not to walk back on the track.

When you return to the dog bring him to the starting place, which your helper has marked. Quietly unsnap the long line and let it lie on the ground for now.

*Note: How to release a dog on any kind of track

When releasing a dog on any track (of a dead or wounded bird) you should first unsnap his leash. Then grasp his collar with your left hand, bend over and point down at the ground with your right finger towards the release spot where the dead bird first hit the ground, and where your helper marked the spot. When you begin with the pointing finger, put your finger right in front of the dog's face so that he actually watches your finger and hand move down, pointing toward the ground at the start of the track. Following your pointing finger and hand gets him to lower his head immediately and focus on the track.

Pointing your finger toward the ground will always be the dog's visual signal that there is something to find on the ground. He will come to understand that the quicker he lowers his head the quicker he will find the game. While pointing to the release spot give the command "fetch."

If the dog is successful do one more track. Then quit for the day. If the dog is not successful, move to a different spot and try again, making the drag shorter and easier.

Photo 1. *This demonstrates how much the pointing finger or hand gets the dog's nose down quickly. It teaches the dog to follow your <u>visual</u> clue and the dog is happy to have this support. In this photo the handler has just gotten the dog's head down. (Compliments Tina Molt.)*

Photo 2. *This handler has used the pointing hand to guide his dog onto the start of the track and he has just let go of the collar. (Compliments Rem DeJong.)*

Photo 3. *This dog is so hot on the track that the handler has barely had time to let go! (Compliments Jerry Yeast.)*

Step 3. *Extending the drag track and ending out of the dog's sight.*

The dog should have the training collar on. First, do a refresher track for the dog—Step 2, the short, "out of sight" retrieve. If the dog fails to do this, go back to Step 1 and lay a drag track ending in sight of the dog. Then do exercise two again, with the track *ending out of sight of the dog.*

If the "out of sight" retrieve (Step 2) is successful, and 99 percent of the time it is, during step 3 keep lengthening the distance of the tracks. Any time the dog makes a mistake, go back one step.

Keep changing objects to be retrieved—different kinds of dead game, dummies (and different weight dummies so the dog begins to build up his muscles for retrieving a heavy object from 150 yards). Sometimes use something other than game---your hat, your glove, any object that the dog is familiar with. *Go to lots of different places to do drags.* Keep making the drags longer until he is retrieving properly up to 150 yards.

End each training session on a positive note, with the dog succeeding. If necessary go back a step to something the dog knows well and allow him to be successful before ending the lesson.

Step 3 should be done over a period of a few weeks. Each day builds on the previous work. Plan your own schedule so that you can work with the dog every day. It's important that you do drag tracks in lots of different places.

Caution: Although most dogs enjoy doing drag tracks, it's easy to do too many during one training session; the dog can easily go sour on you. Only do a couple each day while you are training for this. You can do one drag today, and tomorrow do two, and skip a day now and then. Mix it up.

When you progress to doing a long drag track, one track a day is enough, followed by a run lasting however much time you have. Even a 10 minute run is heaven for a dog. Remember at the end of every session, *immediately pet him, roughhouse a little, tell him how brilliant he is and so on.* (No one but you and the dog are there so you don't have to worry about looking and sounding a bit strange!)

Retrieving from a drag track seems like a simple thing, and in some ways it is, but it asks quite a bit of a dog: to follow a track a long distance and then *go out of the Boss's sight.* For the dog this means he is away from the security of the pack. Drag tracks help the dog build confidence in himself so he will be more reliable in his retrieving duties. Picture a wounded duck that swims into thick reeds out of sight. The dog must not only be well trained to retrieve, but also experienced in performing some of his tasks out of the Boss's sight. Retrieving from a drag track helps the dog build confidence in himself and at the same time builds cooperation between him and you. It builds the team, or in dog talk it strengthens the pack.

Training for retrieving from a drag track is very important and the dog must be successful.

Step 4. *Enforcing the command "fetch."*

Continue increasing the distance of the drag tracks, and continue doing them in different places. When you feel the dog is completely trained to do this task, get someone to help you lay a track on which the dog can't succeed. The helper drags the dead game 150 yards, ending out of the dog's sight. *He does not leave the game on the ground, but instead puts it up in a tree or some high spot, so there is no way for the dog to get the game.* Eventually, the dog will come back without the game.

While the dog is on the way back to you, the helper lays the game on the ground exactly where the track ended. Then he quickly walks away and hides downwind from the dog. *We don't want the dog to find the helper.* If he does, the helper remains still with his back to the dog and does not say a word.

In the meantime the dog has reached you. Put the dog at heel, give the command "fetch" again, with a little more authority in your voice, and point down at the ground where the track started. Then release the dog. He should follow the drag track again, reach the game, pick it up and race back to you, relieved he was able to do the job. This step helps to reinforce for the dog that *he must retrieve the game when he is sent.* This may be the only time in the dog's life when you deliberately set him up to fail, but it's a tremendous tool for exacting success in retrieving wounded game.

Step 5. *Have other people lay drag tracks.*

Have a couple of different friends who know about drag tracks, meet you in the field or woods. Keep the dog in your car and have the friend lay a drag track that ends out of sight. As soon as he gives a shout, blows his whistle, or whatever the signal is that the track has been laid and he is hiding, bring the dog up and start him on the track.

The reason for this is to get the dog used to retrieving from a drag track *no matter who lays it.* Do this step with more than one person unknown to the dog. It also helps ensure success if you plan to enter him in a field test. He needs to learn that he must always complete the retrieve, no matter who laid it.

Using a drag track to find game is not a test of the dog's nose or scenting ability. Almost any dog from a pound would do just as well in finding the game as one of our hunting dogs. This is because the track that we leave from our boots plus the dragged game leaves a very strong scent.

For our dogs this allows them to learn how to use a track to find game, and also teaches the dog to *concentrate* on the track in order to reach the game and to do so *out of sight of the Boss.* This is retrieving training, not a test of the dog's nose, even though he has to use his nose to do the job.

Photo 4. *This German Shorthair is completing a retrieve from a drag track with a dead raccoon! A little unusual but for training purposes it works. Most of the versatile breeds love to retrieve fur so it's okay to use dead rabbits, squirrels, whatever you have. I've known some folks to pick up a road kill that wasn't smashed up. (Compliments Warren Webster.)*

Photo 5. *Training for drag tracks makes a better retriever as this dog proudly shows us. (Compliments Tina Molt.)*

CHAPTER NINE

Stay at the Spot*
Building Confidence

STAY AT THE SPOT is yet another way for gaining more control over your hunting dog. It's also useful in certain hunting scenarios when you may want to leave him, for example, while you creep up to the edge of a pond to check for ducks. And sometimes you need to leave him, go off somewhere and fire your gun, but you need your dog to stay where you left him.

It may sound like a difficult thing to train a dog to stay at the spot, but actually it's not that hard *if your dog is already trained to the drop, and also trained to retrieve from a drag track.* In chapter two on obedience your dog was trained to sit and stay, even with distractions. Stay at the spot is just an extension of that in the field. It is another step toward having him under control at all times.

As you train for stay at the spot and as your dog succeeds in this exercise you will find he becomes much steadier at the duck blind, AND you can stop him if he breaks on a flushed bird.

*First appeared in the *Pointing Dog Journal,* January/February 1995, as *Steady To Wing & Shot Made Easier* by Joan Bailey. This is a revised version. Grateful acknowledgment to PDJ for permission to use it.

Before attempting to train your dog to stay at the spot he should be *100 percent comfortable with being shot over. Do not attempt stay at the spot training until after the dog's first hunting season when a good number of birds have been shot over him.*

Note: Remember that your dog is now already trained to the "drop." As you proceed through the training for "stay at the spot," any time the dog breaks (gets up, walks away, tries to follow you), put him back on the "spot" and make him "drop." As soon as he succeeds in a step, switch back to "sit." Or, you can make him drop first, then put him back on the spot and give him "sit." It depends on you and the dog.

Step 1. *The dog stays sitting beside the vest while you walk around him.*

This work should first be done in a fenced in yard, then moved to the field.

In the yard the dog wears the pinch collar and you use the short, over-the-shoulder leash (or just a short leash if you don't have the over-the-shoulder kind). Your dog is already trained to sit and stay on command, even with distractions. Start by giving the "sit" command and walk a short distance out of his sight. Return in 10-15 seconds. This step is like a quick refresher course for him to remember he must sit and stay until released by a command.

After putting the dog at "sit," place a piece of your clothing you are wearing (hunting vest or jacket) beside him. Be sure the item is actually touching the dog. (See Photo 1.)

1. At first it's best to back away from the dog, keeping eye contact as a means of enforcing the command.

2. Slowly stroll around him, making sure he stays sitting.

3. Next, hold the leash and begin walking slowly in a circle around him, giving him the idea he must stay where you put him—beside the clothing—until you release him.

If he moves off the sit at any time (stands up, tries to walk) correct him by putting him back on the exact spot and commanding him to sit. This is similar to the basic obedience training, the "sit" (in chapter 2, Photo 2.) but without the switch because the dog already knows this command.

When he is successful go to him, praise him, and pick up your clothing. Release him with another command: "come," or "heel." *This is very important, don't omit this step.* Immediately praise him again.

This step should have taken you no more than five minutes. If you are successful do two more, exactly the same, but in different places—maybe your front yard or another place in the backyard. Any time the dog attempts to leave the spot, go back and put him in the original place.

This fist step should be accomplished the first day, but if not, continue the next day. Remember: Do not allow the training session to last more than 10 minutes, and you must end with success. If it takes two days or more, that's okay.

Photo 1. *Tell the dog to "Stay," take off your vest or jacket and put it next to the dog so that it is actually touching him. (All photos for this chapter by the author.)*

Step 2. *Working on the long line*

Change to the long line and keep doing the same as in step 1, increasing the distance between you and the dog until you have the line played out all the way.

In both Step 1 and Step 2, *don't do the exercise more than two or three times at the most in one training session,* even if it takes you more days. Also, mix up the training sessions a bit to avoid boredom. Go to the water and do a little retrieving (no more than 2 retrieves), or go out and do one retrieve from a drag track, *always ending on a positive note.*

Step 3. *Dropping the leash and going out of sight of the dog.*

First do Step 2 again to make sure the dog has not forgotten overnight. As soon as he is doing this consistently, begin dropping the leash in front of him and continue moving to all sides and behind him. *Remember to put a piece of your clothing beside him immediately after you command him to sit.* Always correct him if he makes a mistake. The time when he is most apt to stand up and turn around to find you is when he can't see you.

Go out of the dog's sight. You can go around the side of your house, but you must find a place where you can peek and observe him. Be sure the wind will not take your scent to him. He will be looking in the area where he last saw you, so you must observe him from a different location. You have to plan out locations ahead of time so you know exactly where to go. The instant he moves from the spot, you must go to him and correct him by putting him back exactly where he was. *Depending on the dog, you may have to put him in the "drop" until you get past this part of the training.*

It's critical that you change directions and places frequently so that the dog does not catch on to your "hiding" technique. You can only use the same place once or twice because the dog figures out that you are watching him; you'll need to change locations often. For the first day you may need two locations lined up. Maybe a neighbor's yard or an empty school yard.

Never call the dog to you. Always go back to him. This builds the dog's confidence in you. He knows you will always come back to him. And, *always leave a piece of clothing, and always pick it up when you return to the dog.* Do not walk him away with the clothing left behind. We want the piece of clothing to become a kind of anchor for the dog.

Proceed gradually: leave the dog and be out of his sight for 15 seconds, then 30 seconds, one minute, two minutes, three minutes, and so on.

Step 4. *Distractions.*

Once the dog is staying at the spot consistently for three minutes, begin introducing distractions such as slamming a door, rolling a bone in front of him, and finally firing a shot. All these distractions should be done first in front of him where you can maintain eye contact and control. This is especially so when you fire the first shot!

For the first shot stand no more than 20 feet from the dog. Look directly at him when you shoot. If he attempts to stand up, make him drop. If you can't fire a gun in your neighborhood, use a blank pistol. In the field use a shotgun.

The dog will want to see you and will often stand up and look for you. You want to have a bond with him, and still have him trust that you will return and praise him for a job well done. You must use great care when correcting him.

Step 5. *Stay at the spot in the field.*

Now your training is all in the field. You'll have to find suitable areas to continue the lessons. In the beginning in the field, put the dog on sit, drop your vest or coat beside him and walk out of sight into woods or behind tall bushes, whatever kind of cover you've got *that's not too far away.*

Photo 2. *The dog should "stay at the spot," waiting for the handler to return.*

The first time you shoot in the field out of sight of the dog, just step into the woods and fire the shot. Step back in sight immediately and walk back to him. Praise him quietly and be sure you pick up your vest (Photo 3). Then give him a command, such as heel, to release him from "Stay At the Spot" and walk away (Photo 4). If it was successful, do it again exactly the same way but stay out of sight for 30 seconds after the shot, then go back to the dog. That's enough for this session. Take the dog for a run, or do something fun for both of you.

On subsequent days increase your hiding time very gradually: 30 seconds, one minute, two minutes, three minutes and up to six minutes. Keep increasing the distance up to 150 yards out of sight. The first time in the field go only 30 yards before cutting into the woods, and only stay one minute. Then return to the dog, pick up the vest and give lavish praise, tell the dog to heel and walk away. (See Photos 3 and 4.)

If that was successful, try another one in a different area and go farther away from the dog, say 50 yards and hide for two minutes.

If successful, that is all you should do this day. Go out the next day, to a new place, do the same thing but stay hidden longer, three to four minutes.

Photo 3. *Pick up the vest; give a quiet "good boy," and a command to release him from "staying at the spot," such as come or heel.*

Photo 4. *Walk away with the dog at heel. Do another lesson or go for a run.*

Continue for the next days, gradually increasing the distance and hiding time, being sure to make small, gradual increases. It may take several weeks. Eventually you should be able to leave the dog, walk 150 yards out of sight, fire a shot, wait 15 seconds, then fire again, then walk back to the dog and quietly praise him. That is the final goal.

Continue going to different places, but don't do the "stay at a spot" every day. Take a break every so often so the dog doesn't get bored, or tired of the training. Work on something else once in a while.

Throughout training for "stay at the spot" it's important that any time the dog disobeys—gets up or leaves the spot he must be punished. The easiest punishment for both you and the dog is to give the "drop" command and insist that he keep his head on the ground between his front feet, even when you walk out of sight. He won't like it, he will be uncomfortable with that but he must learn to obey at all times. As soon as he is staying on the spot, you can begin having him sit again. If he disobeys again, put him on the drop. *Never hit the dog.* Use only the methods described here. If you hit the dog, he will learn to distrust you, and you will have lost your edge in training and in having a great dog.

Again, the same reminder: end every training session with a successful performance by the dog. Then lavish praise and take him for a run in the field if possible, or just a ride to the store, anything that is special for him and done with you.

CHAPTER TEN

Steady at the Blind

WE WANT OUR DOG to be rock solid steady in a duck blind, or any kind of blind. This kind of steady means: staying at the sit, or down, not whining, and staying absolutely quiet and still.

If your dog is absolutely rock solid trained to the "drop" you can proceed to steady at the blind. Wait at least one month after you have completed the training for drop before you start steady at the blind. Keep working your dog on all other aspects of his training (stay at the spot, retrieve from drag track), using a lot of runs in different places where you can reinforce the "drop." Do the "drop" maybe only once during an outing and at different times during each run: five minutes after you've been out, next time in the middle of the run, next time five minutes before you're ready to quit. These changes will keep it fresh for the dog, and reinforced in his memory bank. Do it in lots of different places.

Your dog should also be well conditioned to the gun by this time so when you fire it beside a pond it will not frighten him. He should have had plenty of experience chasing a shackled duck in a shallow pond (See Chapter 5), as well as having enough birds shot over him in the field and woods so that he is now conditioned and oriented to look where a bird is flying, see that it's hit, and see where it falls.

If your dog has not been through his first hunting season, skip this chapter and do it the following spring.

Working with Decoys

Step 1. *Navigating decoys.*

Put out a bunch of decoys on your lawn, spreading them a bit as you would in the water. Have the dog at the sit and let him watch you. After the decoys are set out, place a dummy close to the edge of the decoys where the dog can't miss it. Go back to the dog and give the "fetch." If he goes past the dummy call him back and start over. If he still misses the dummy, walk to him and show him the dummy. Do this in a joyful way as a helper, not in a disciplinary way. Or, for the first time have him on the short lead. Walk him at heel to the dummy, say "fetch," and have him carry the dummy back to the starting place. Be sure he picks up the dummy correctly, and returns and delivers it properly to you. Don't forget the praise when he does it correctly.

Do this several times, putting the dummy on different sides of the decoys. After he has done these retrieves successfully, place the dummy in the middle of the decoys. Correct him whenever he makes a mistake (picking up a decoy instead of the dummy). This is just correction, not punishment. Showing the dog what you require. At first he may not understand that he should retrieve the dummy. So if he picks up a decoy, make the correction in a kind way by showing him you want the dummy, not the decoy. Then, when you start using a dead duck he will know what he is suppose to retrieve.

When he is successful substitute a dead bird for the dummy. A dead duck would be best, but any dead game bird will be okay. At the same time increase the distance: have the dog sit farther away so he has a longer distance to go both out and back.

Step 1 can be done in one, two, or three training sessions. And, remember *to keep each session to ten minutes.*

When the dog has had many successes retrieving different objects from among the decoys, and if you are an avid goose hunter, this is a good time to use a heavier dummy as preparation for when the dog will carry a heavy goose while swimming in the water and then out onto land.

Step 2: *Water retrieving from decoys in shallow water.*

Now go to a pond, as described in Chapter 5. Set up some kind of blind. It doesn't have to be fancy, but it should be realistic, something close to what you would use in a real hunting situation. A field green or camouflage tarp will do, with two 6-foot poles set up on the edge of the shallow pond for the dog to sit beside, or behind, *providing he can see.*

Set some decoys out in shallow water, not swimming depth if possible. If it's not that shallow it's okay, but the non swimming depth is better in the beginning for building the dog's confidence. We want to make it as comfortable and secure as possible for him to succeed. This particular training step is mentally and emotionally hard on the dog, so having the shallow water helps to promote confidence in the dog during this training.

If it is swimming depth it should not be very deep. See page 52 for best depth. With the decoys set out in shallow water the strings attached to the decoys do not have to be long so there is less chance of the dog getting tangled.

For the first few times don't put out many decoys—use just a few at first, which allows the dog to get used to the strings without getting tangled. If he swims into a short string he can usually figure out how to get away from it, which is something he has to learn on his own from this kind of experience. Later you can gradually go into deeper water to give him more opportunity to learn about the strings. When he's successful in the deep water, add more decoys.

This step will take more than one 10 minute session. It will take a few sessions. Be careful that the dog doesn't get tired or stressed. Plan that you will need several days before the dog is completely trained to be steady during this work.

Step 3. *Building confidence in retrieving from water through exposure.*

Over a period of two or three weeks go to the pond, set the decoys and give the dog practice in retrieving different objects from water. Make it interesting, use different kinds of dead birds and use a different kind of dummy once in a while.

Make sure all retrieves are done properly, and no putting the bird down at the edge of the water to shake. *One or two successful retrieves in one day is quite adequate. Don't go to the pond every day.* In between do something else like field work and be sure the dog has a daily run.

Steady at the Blind

Soft dogs: If you have a soft dog you should skip the steady at the blind work. It's too much emotional and mental pressure for a soft dog. He will probably collapse under this kind of pressure. You can do the retrieving from among the decoys, but just don't do any shooting. Don't try to train your soft dog to be steady at the blind with gunfire.

Step 1. *Using a shackled duck to teach dog not to break at the shot.*

The dog is now completely comfortable with the blind, with the decoys and with retrieving dead ducks from the decoys. You will need a helper for this, and a live, shackled duck. Do this work at a small pond with at least a little cover at the edges. Set out decoys off to the side a bit, not directly in front of the blind.

Have your helper go along the edge of the pond a good distance from you and the dog, but very visible to the dog. Your helper has the shackled duck which is attached to light string. You and the dog are beside the blind, the dog at "sit" and wearing the pinch collar.

On a signal from you your helper throws the duck (which is still attached to the light rope) into the water about 8 or 10 feet from shore and allows it to splash around. If the dog makes any attempt to break—even the slightest movement—you must quickly use the pinch collar (a couple of jerks on the leash) and immediately give the "drop" command. Insist on the proper position. Your helper pulls in the duck while you correct the dog. After 60 seconds, release him from the drop by saying "Sit."

Now repeat everything again. At the dog's slightest movement order the "drop" and insist on the proper position. Release the dog from the drop by saying "sit." Usually by the 3rd or 4th attempt, the dog will remain steady when the duck is thrown into the water, and will remain steady as the duck swims and thrashes around.

Step 2. *Retrieving the duck as a reward.*

When the dog is absolutely steady, instruct your helper to remove the rope from the duck and to toss the duck out again. Let the duck swim 30 to 60 seconds. Then give the dog the command "fetch."

For this particular session his first retrieve with a live duck from decoys, you should stand one step into the water so that you can meet him and prevent him from putting the duck down, and help him be successful. Taking the duck while the dog is still in the water usually prevents him from shaking. (They almost always wait until they are out of the water to shake.) If this retrieve is successful and you've just taken the duck, give lavish praise. Then take him for a run. This exercise acts as a reward for the dog, he gets to go after the duck, catch it and bring it to you.

The next time you go to the pond to do water work, instead of standing in the water, stand at the very edge of the pond. Repeat everything above. The next time stand one step back from shore.

Each time you work on this, stand back another step until you are about eight or nine feet from the edge and the dog is retrieving the duck to hand every time. Any time he makes a mistake--puts the duck down to shake--go to him, correct him, and then stand closer to the edge of the water for the next retrieve. In correcting your dog (not to put the duck down to shake), try to anticipate this by watching the dog closely. You'll be able to judge his body language and anticipate that he is about to put down the duck. If you observe this you can say another "fetch," which often prevents the dog from making the mistake. During the next retrieve, whether it is the same day, or the next, he may observe your intent to correct him and he may not put down the duck. If that happens give praise as soon as he delivers the duck to hand. *Every day that he is successful with a water retrieve take him for a run after you're finished.*

Don't go to the water every day. Do something different, or just go out for a run—no training. With this training it's important not to work too much at the water. Every other day is good. And find at least one different place to do this training so the dog understands he has to do this work anywhere.

Step 3. *Introducing the gun with water retrieves.*

Continue practicing some retrieving from water with dummies and dead birds. Begin introducing a little shooting once in a while so the dog connects this scenario with hunting. Your helper can throw a dead duck out and you can shoot, making the dog remain steady until given the command to "fetch."

The first time you do a retrieve for steady at the blind with gunfire without the leash leave the pinch collar on the dog. It will give you a psychological edge because the dog will feel the collar which he associates with you being in control of him.

Photo 1. *After one or two successful retrieves when he remains steady with gunfire, remove the collar. If the dog gets sloppy put the collar back on. (Author training for steady at the blind. Compliments Vern Brand.)*

Photo 2. *Experienced and fully trained dog completing a retrieve from deep water during a full Utility Field Test for versatile hunting dogs. You can tell that she hasn't shook or put the duck down. The duck is going straight to her boss. (Compliments Allan Russell.)*

Step 4. *Hand signals.*

Now you can begin to introduce a few basic hand signals. Throw a stone where you want the dog to go, followed immediately with the command "back." He will soon associate the command to mean to go farther. Gradually let the throwing arm be the signal, without throwing a stone. You can also use this to teach the dog to go to the left or right.

Be sure you give the dog enough opportunities for retrieving dead birds among the decoys. More experience is better than not enough when you are actually hunting waterfowl, so he won't try to pick up a decoy to retrieve.

The versatile breeds and pointers and setters depend on their scenting and searching abilities to find downed waterfowl more than do the retrieving specialists. But it's very helpful for them to know a few basic retrieving signals for waterfowl hunting. For retrievers, the specialists in water retrieving, check out the fine books available on this subject.

Note: If you jump shoot ducks when you're out for upland birds, and you don't hunt ducks from a blind, you don't need to train for this, unless you want to qualify your dog in a field test.

Chapter Eleven

Steady to Wing and Shot Made Easier

STEADY TO WING means that when the dog has pointed a bird, he will not break when you walk in to flush the bird, or when the bird flies. The dog allows you to do your job. Steady to shot means that the dog will not break after the shot even if the bird is dropped. Quail hunters know there is often a lagging bird in the covey, and you don't want the dog in the way of a delayed shot after the first flush.

There have always been different opinions on whether a dog should be steady to wing and shot. Some hunters want their dog to be steady to wing, but not to shot. Many hunters want their dogs to go on the shot because they feel time is a critical factor in retrieving crippled birds (especially a wing-tipped pheasant). If a dog is steady to wing and has let you flush the bird he can see the direction the bird has taken; if you have knocked down the bird, he sees that too. If he goes immediately after the shot, he may have the advantage of getting to the bird sooner than if he waits to be told to "fetch." It's an age-old discussion and we won't settle it here.

Steady to wing (and flush) alone, though, is a safety issue as well as an aid to finding the game. If the dog is steady to wing, what we really mean is that the dog is steady to *flush*. You walk in, flush the bird, the dog *holds and watches the bird*, you drop the bird and the

101

dog takes off to get it. It's been safe for you to shoot without possibly hitting the dog and the dog gets to see the direction of the bird (unless you're in very high cover), so there is a better chance of recovery.

If you want your dog to be steady to flush, it's quite easy to teach him *after* he is trained to the drop. You can do it while hunting, or by using a couple of planted birds. With planted birds (pen raised birds) the dog may not point them especially if he's been hunted on wild birds. He may perceive them to be wounded. (Pen-raised birds have a stronger scent due to being held in captivity in a small area with other birds such as a small pen, a crate etc. Due to this they don't smell like a wild bird, and their scent is much stronger.) If that's the case, do this exercise two or three times and he should get the message that he is to point that kind of bird as well as wild ones. You're teaching him to point pen-raised birds, and that's okay. It won't affect his ability when he's in real hunting situations.

You'll have to use a long line and use the wind to work him into the bird. He may perceive the pen-raised bird as being wounded and start to move in to retrieve it. This is where the long line can prevent that, and teach him to point the pen-raised birds.

Step 1. *Teaching your dog to point a pen raised bird.*

First find strong-flying birds from a good source. See Appendix and ask your hunting friends. As with the duck work get the birds (pheasants or chukars) close to the day you plan to do this training so the birds are fresh and haven't been confined in a crate for very long.

You will need at least one helper, maybe two. Instruct them how you want the birds to be planted. (Gently swing the bird back and forth, then tuck the head under a wing and place it in a likely spot, and leave a marker like a piece of orange ribbon on a nearby bush.).

Attach a long line (at least 20 feet) to the dog's collar. Release him in the direction of the planted bird. Allow him to work with the line dragging behind him. Keep up with him, staying back a bit but close enough so that you can get to him quickly. Instruct your helper to stay twenty feet behind you. That way he won't be a distraction to the dog.

Watch the dog carefully and as soon as you see that he's got a whiff of the bird (getting "birdy"), get up there quickly, take hold of the long line and carefully work your way up the line, hand over hand until you are close to the dog. As you pick up the line and start working to get close to the dog you can speak quietly to him—perhaps "whoa" a few times. (He should remember "whoa" from his early conditioning.) So far all he knows is that there's a wounded bird there and he wants to get it. He's doing everything he should be doing, don't discipline him in any way, but rather continue to teach him to do something that is not natural: pointing the pen-raised bird.

Having the dog on the long line allows you to quietly slow him down and restrain him from going in and scooping up the bird. When you are close to him continue to hold the line in one hand and with the other hand, stroke him softly from the top of his head to the tip of his tail. Run your hand under his tail. As you stroke him he may begin to sense what you are asking of him, and his body should begin to become a little rigid as he begins to point with some intensity. As this happens, quietly say "whoa," continue running your hand from his head to the tip of his tail. Two or three times is plenty. A quiet "good boy" can help.

Have your helper walk out in front of the dog and flush the bird while you stay beside the dog to keep it from chasing. Don't come down hard on him, because he has just learned something new. *Great care must be taken when working with a dog on point.* Everything must be done in the most positive way, ending with much praise.

Try this step on at least two more outings. If all goes well by this time the dog will be pointing the planted bird. Then you can proceed to the next step.

Photo 1. *Both photos taken during a field test by the author. The dogs were hunted on wild birds. Both dogs were taught to point pen-raised, planted birds. The handler is walking in from directly behind the dog instead of coming in more from the side.*

Photo 2. *The handler comes in from an angle which is much more supportive of the dog and in a hunting condition more productive. German Shorthair above, German Wirehair below.*

Step 2. *Steady to flush.*

You will need a helper for this step. If you are using a planted bird, work the dog into the bird, being sure to use the wind correctly. Have your two-tone whistle with the large end in your mouth. When he goes on point walk in and flush the bird. The *moment* the dog moves off point or even starts to move, blow the whistle and say "drop." Using two different commands for the same job is double enforcement. Go to him and say "come," and leash him. Have him heel until you reach the next area where a bird was planted, then work him into the bird. Walk in and flush the bird. If he starts to move use the drop immediately. Make sure he goes all the way down with his head on his paws or between his feet.

The dog will want to stand up to see where the bird goes and where it lands, which is fine in a hunting situation. But during this phase of training you must insist on the drop. Later, during a field test situation, because he will be trained to point and hold planted birds you won't need to make him drop: thus he will be able to watch the bird and see where it lands.

Do this step a third time; he should hold steady to flush. If he is successful, take him for a good run. If he's not successful, go back a step until you can move forward to this exercise.

If you don't want to use planted birds, however, go where you know birds should be and work the dog as if you were hunting wild birds. When he goes on point move in and walk past him, keeping your eyes on him while you flush the bird. Then do exactly as above: blow the "drop" end of the whistle, and go through the same steps. It will take longer than using planted birds, but it can be done. It may take two or three outings until you find enough birds to complete this step. The planted birds will give you more control of the situation, and fewer surprises.

Steady to Shot

Training for steady to shot requires you have someone with you to do the shooting which frees you to concentrate 100 percent on working with the dog. The shooter must know exactly when to shoot. You and he must work out the logistics before you start.

Step 1. *Working the dog into the first bird and shooting.*

If you want your dog to be steady to shot, as well as to flush, it's not too difficult *once he is trained to steady to wing/flush,* and *after he is trained to the drop.* Just as in steady to flush, you can use planted or wild birds, but with steady to shot using planted birds is better because you can set everything up, and neither you nor the dog will be confused or surprised.

Have your helper plant a bird in 3 different places so you can work the dog from one bird, to the next, and to the third.

Decide before you start how you want to do this (pointing, flushing, shooting). Do you want your helper to walk out in front of the dog and flush the bird so you can stay beside the dog and concentrate on him? And do you want him to do the shooting? If you let him do these two things you'll be able to concentrate 100 percent on the dog. I suggest that you do it this way. With all your efforts directed at the dog your chance of success is greater. Later you can transition and become the flusher and shooter.

You and the helper work the dog into the first bird, using the wind properly. Don't be surprised if your dog uses the planter's track to locate the bird. The important thing is how he handles the bird after the flush. He is already steady to flush. When he goes on point your helper should come from the side if possible and walk confidently out in front of the dog in the direction his nose is pointed. Keep your whistle in your mouth and concentrate on the dog. The helper should move along and flush the bird, and make a good shot and drop it.

Another way is to have the helper off to the side a bit and you walk in and flush the bird and the helper shoots. Just be sure you both know which plan before you start.

The dog has no doubt broken to shot because he hasn't been taught anything different up until now. This is why you must be very alert and ready. The moment he breaks after the shot, blow the drop command on the whistle. Make sure he drops immediately and that he takes the proper position—front legs out in front of him, head on his legs. Let him stay like that for up to one minute. Then go to him, clip on the leash and have him sit beside your left knee for 30 seconds.

Then, being sure the dog is facing in the correct direction, send him to retrieve the downed bird. After a proper retrieve, with praise, work him into another planted bird and insist on him staying steady after the shot. If he breaks, give the "drop" command. Then do the retrieve. *Remember to praise for a proper retrieve.*

Step 2. *Working the third bird and enforcing steady to shot.*

This is a complete repeat of Step 1, except this time you don't know what the dog will do when you shoot. When he goes on point do everything as above. If he breaks completely repeat what you did before.

If he starts to break, blow the drop at any movement and insist on the proper position. After one or two minutes go to him and give minimal praise like a short pat on the head with a quiet "good boy." Then send him to retrieve the downed bird. As soon as he retrieves the bird properly to you give him a lot of praise.

Leash the dog and walk toward the next area. Release him and work him into the next bird. Walk in on the point, flush the bird and shoot it. Now he may not move. If so, go to him and say "Fetch."

When he returns with the bird and makes a proper retrieve to you, give him a lot of praise as soon as you take the bird from him.

You *must* take him for a run now. Perhaps in the fields where you have been working. This has been a huge accomplishment and deserves a lot of reward (praise and a run).

Step 3. *Continue to enforce steady to shot.*

Go out the next day while yesterday's experience is still fresh in the dog's mind. But, *go to a different field. If you go to the same field he will remember where the birds were yesterday and go to those areas.*

Do everything as in step 2 and expect him to be steady to shot. If not, use the whistle and the voice command "drop." Insist on the proper position. Then have him do the retrieve. Then go to yet another planted bird; it should now be cemented in his mind that he must not break at the shot.

If you are into field trials or field testing, where steady to wing and shot are required, this is how you can do it. In a versatile hunting dog test, you could qualify your dog, but not with a Prize I. That would require steady to flush and shot with no commands. If you are satisfied with a Prize II or III, then this will do it.

Photo 3. *Above, at a Utility Field Test. The dog was hunted on lots of wild birds, and was trained to point planted birds. He knows "this is a game" and he's not intense at all. He's merely "standing the bird," as he has been taught to do while the boss tries to flush the bird.*

Photo 4. *Below, same handler, different dog, different test area, same scenario. The dog's tail is down; he's just "standing the bird." If you took either dog out hunting on wild birds the next day you would see intense points. (Both photos by the author.)*

How to Punish Your Dog Severely
Without Physical Pain

Dr. Tabel reminds us that you can only do this exercise with success *after* your dog is fully trained to the drop. Only use this form of punishment when your dog is deliberating misbehaving, or he won't do a task that he already *knows and understands*. For example, refusing to bring a piece of game to you, then you can punish him this way *(after he is fully trained to drop)*.

Timing is of the essence. Always. To punish too long after the bad behavior does no good. Let's say you sent the dog to retrieve something; he went partway and came back to you, or maybe he went all the way, looked at the dead bird, and decided not to pick it up and bring it back. Rather than waiting for him to come to you, walk toward him and command him to "drop."

When you reach him, attach the leash. Then say come. As he starts to rise, say "drop" and move back a step. Then say "come." As he starts to rise say "drop." Move back another step. Keep doing the "come/drop" moving back a step each time. This maneuver puts the dog into a crawl position, which he hates. Do this for *five or six steps:* "come." "drop" "come." "drop." On the last "come" be sure he sits beside your left leg. Then point in the direction of the dead game and at the same time give the command, "fetch." He will probably take off like a shot, grab the bird and bring it back to you. Give quiet praise.

CHAPTER TWELVE

The Best Trained Hunting Dog

IT'S BEEN MY EXPERIENCE that the methods described in this book will work for anyone who truly wants a fully trained hunting dog, and a well-trained family dog. These steps and lessons require some patience, but not an awful lot. I'm not the most patient person you'll ever meet, yet I found this system works really well for my dogs and me. The patience it does *require is merely doing it in tiny, consistent steps, with determination.* I truly want a well-trained dog and I'm willing to devote 10 minutes a day for three or four months to obtain it. Also, it's fun to have something to do with your dog when it's not hunting season.

Once a dog is fully trained as described here, you will discover that you'll also have a better hunting dog, and that he'll find and retrieve more birds than before. So for three or four months of short lessons every day, you'll end up with a finely tuned, completely trained dog. You and he will bring home a lot of birds over the next twelve years. It's worth the effort.

Another benefit is that during the months of training you'll feel good as you experience your progress. Also, I believe the dog will be happier. I think this is so because first, he thinks you are almost God and he wants to please you, his Boss. So as the training progresses

111

he begins to feel good about himself, about succeeding and pleasing you. And, of course, the pack of you and the dog becomes stronger and stronger. And never forget, *dogs love to learn, especially if they have a benevolent trainer.*

Instructions for Family Members

Assuming you are the man in the family—hunter, the trainer, you must tell other family members—your wife and kids, not to give any of these new commands to the dog until well after the training is completed. If the dog is just learning the sit, stay and heel and a kid gives him one of those commands, there will be no way to enforce it and the dog will have learned *not* to do something you just taught him. The same goes for the entire training period—no fetching, no drop, *nothing from family members except love.* And during the training period *you will be the only person to feed the dog.* You'll probably be unpopular for a few months, but this too shall pass.

Some months after the training is completed you can show and teach family members how to use the commands that can be useful around home. For the first few times you should be present when a family member does this and make sure the dog obeys them, and that they are giving the proper command. Over time the dog will learn that although you are his BOSS other family members have control over him too.

A Bonus for Everyone

If you have young kids at home, after you have completed the training, you can offer to take your dog to a "Show & Tell" day at school. One of my old hunting friends did that in his home town of York, Nebraska. His dog was completely trained and under control at all times. He demonstrated a little of the training and talked a bit about hunting, describing the work his dog was required to do. The kids loved it and wrote him little letters thanking him. Each wanted to have a dog like that some day!

Special Tip

Now that you know a lot more about training a gun dog, please go back to Chapter One and read the list of **Training Tips** again. You know more now so you will understand those tips a lot better than when you started.

The First Dog I Trained Using Dr. Tabel's Methods

A few years after I completed the training of that dog, we had an opportunity to buy a four year old male dog that we wanted to use for breeding, and also we wanted to give him a home where he would be hunted more. After going through the adjustment period of bringing an adult male dog into a home with another adult male, the two males became good buddies. They ate together, slept together, and hung out together.

The new male had not had a lot of training. He knew what whoa meant, but he hadn't been trained to be completely steady. Some days he would whoa and some days he wouldn't. One day when he had been with us for about four months, he and the older dog needed exercise but I had limited time so I took them out together.

We started out in a small open field, working towards the edge of a swamp. As I turned and walked parallel to the swamp the new dog worked in front of me while the older dog went into the middle of the swamp. In a moment I heard a commotion from the swamp. Out came two whitetail deer running hard with the older dog right behind them. The new dog joined in and both my dogs were on the heels of the two deer.

I blew the "drop" as loud as I could. The older dog stopped in his tracks and stood still. Then I yelled "whoa" to the new dog. He stopped too, and both dogs watched as the deer went out of sight. I walked to the new dog and leashed him, then to the older dog. I gave him a "good boy!" and leashed him as well. Then I walked them in a different direction from the deer and after a while released them to continue our outing.

Without the older dog trained to drop, I don't know what would have happened, but I don't think it would have been a positive outcome. That was a moment of good dog work I'll never forget, thanks to Dr. Tabel's teaching.

Photo 1. *Author and her dog during a hunt in Eastern Nebraska. It was a good day.*

GRACKLE CIPERO, *dam of SORA with a goose in the prairie country of Saskatchewan, Canada. (Compliments Joe Schmutz.)*

Appendix

Training equipment resources:

Lion Country Supply (PA) Dogs Unlimited (CO)
www.lcsupply.com   www.dogsunlimited.com
800-662-5202   800-338-3647

Lion Country Supply carries the proper whistle for this type of training (See page 16, Equipment.).

Both Lion Country and Dogs Unlimited have good quality collars and leashes. Each company has a fine reputation in the world of dog training.

How to order a whistle from Germany:

If you want to have a slightly better two tone whistle you can order it from a well known hunting store in Germany, Frankonia. They have a website, but you'd have to understand German to navigate the site. You can order it by phone (011-49-9302-2979), Monday-Friday 11pm to 9am west coast time (8am to 6pm German time). They take Visa or Master card. The person who answers the phone will speak English.

If you want to try to order it by email, you can email them at: export@frankonia.de.

The German word for this type of whistle is "downpfeife" (double ended). They have plastic #102232-24, or elk horn #11331-24. Price is the same, about $18.40 U.S. plus shipping. These prices are from a 2005 catalog, so they may be a little higher now. They ship internationally all the time.

If you ever get to Germany don't miss spending a good part of a day in one of the Frankonia stores. Their stores are in most good size cities. It's a fantastic experience.

Sources for birds:

Contact the North American Gamebird Association at: 1-800-624-2967 or www.mynaga.org. You'll be able to find shooting preserves in your area. You may be able to buy birds from them, or they may be able to direct you to local sources.

You can also do an online search and find a listing of game bird farms in every state. When you find a few in your area, start asking your hunting friends if they can recommend any of them. Visit and see how they keep their birds. You want a place that has a flight pen. That's a huge wired pen, big enough so birds can fly around a bit. The flight pen helps to produce birds that will be strong flyers and that is exactly what you want.

For ducks try to find a place that maintains the ducks with little human contact. If there is a lot of human contact it's difficult to get the ducks to swim away from you once you release them. But if that's all you can find you'll have to make do by throwing rocks just behind the duck, shouting, waving your hands. Or bring an experienced leashed dog to the edge of the water and his barking should help scare the duck.

As a last resort you may have to pay to do the steady to wing and shot at the preserve.

Bibliography & Suggested Reading

Bailey, Joan. *How to Help Gun Dogs Train Themselves*. Portland: Swan Valley Press, 2008.

Lorenz, Konrad. *Man Meets Dog*. Baltimore: Penquin Books, 1971.

McConnell, Patricia B. *The Other End of the Leash*. New York: Ballantine Book, 2003.

Phaffenberger, Clarence. *The New Knowledge of Dog Behavior*. New York: Howell, 1963.

Scott, John Paul & John L Fuller. *Dog Behavior, the Genetic Basis*. Chicago & London: University of Chicago Press, 1956.

Tabel, Carl. *Der Jagdgebrauchshund*. Munich: F.C. Mayer Druck, 1964. (Later edition, Munich: BLV Verlagsgesellschaft mbH, 1973.)

Trumler, Eberhard. *Your Dog and You*. New York. Seabury Press, 1973. Out of print, but worth a search by a good book store. Or, your local libray can do an inter library search and loan.

(**Note:** These are primarily books about the behavior of dogs. There are hundreds of books about training dogs and they can be found online and in catalogs. The more you understand why your dog behaves as he does, the easier it is for you to train him—and then it is easier for your dog to take to the training.

Five of the above books are quite old, but they are the basis of most of the more recent books about canine behavior.)